Jim Burns's work represents his integrity, intelligence, and his heart for kids. The *Uncommon* high school group studies will change some lives and save many others.

stephen arterburn
Bestselling Author, *Every Man's Battle*

Jim Burns knows kids, understands kids and writes youth curriculum that youth workers, both volunteer and professional, can use.

ridge burns
President, God's Kids (www.godskids.org)

Jim Burns has found the right balance between learning God's Word and applying it to life. The topics are relevant, up to date and on target. Jim gets kids to think. This is a terrific series, and I highly recommend it.

les j. christie
Chair of Youth Ministry, William Jessup University, Rocklin, California

There are very few people in the world who know how to communicate life-changing truth effectively to teens. Jim Burns is one of the best. These studies are biblically sound, hands-on practical and just plain fun. This one gets a five-star endorsement.

ken davis
Author and Speaker (www.kendavis.com)

I don't know anyone who knows and understands the needs of the youth worker like Jim Burns. The *Uncommon* high school group studies are solid, easy to use and get students out of their seats and into the Word.

doug fields
President, Simply Youth Ministry (www.simplyyouthministry.com)

The practicing youth worker always needs more ammunition. The *Uncommon* high school group studies will get that blank stare off the faces of the kids at your youth meeting!

jay kesler
President Emeritus, Taylor University, Upland, Indiana

D0957305

In the *Uncommon* high school group studies, Jim Burns pulls together the key ingredients for an effective series. He captures the combination of teen involvement and a solid biblical perspective with topics that are relevant and straightforward. This will be a valuable tool in the local church.

dennis "tiger" mcluen
Executive Director, Youth Leadership (www.youthleadership.com)

Young people need the information necessary to make wise decisions related to everyday problems. The *Uncommon* high school group studies will help many young people integrate their faith into everyday life, which, after all, is our goal as youth workers.

miles mcpherson
Senior Pastor, The Rock Church, San Diego, California

This is a resource that is user-friendly, learner-centered and intentionally biblical. I love having a resource like this that I can recommend to youth ministry volunteers and professionals.

duffy robbins
Professor of Youth Ministry, Eastern University, St. Davids, Pennsylvania

The *uncommon* high school group studies provide the motivation and information for leaders and the types of experience and content that will capture high school people. I recommend it highly.

denny rydberg
President, Young Life (www.younglife.org)

Jim Burns has done it again! This is a practical, timely and reality-based resource for equipping teens to live life in the fast-paced, pressure-packed adolescent world of today.

rich van pelt
President, Alongside Consulting, Denver, Colorado

Jim Burns has his finger on the pulse of youth today. He understands their mindsets and has prepared these studies in a way that will capture their attention and lead them to greater maturity in Christ.

rick warren
Senior Pastor, Saddleback Church, Lake Forest, California
Author of *The Purpose Driven Life*

high school group study

jim burns
general editor

the new testament

Published by Gospel Light
Ventura, California, U.S.A.
www.gospellight.com
Printed in the U.S.A.

© 1996, 2010 Jim Burns. All rights reserved.
Opening introductions for units written by Jim Burns. Opening devotions
for sessions written by Doug Webster.

Originally published as *The Word on the New Testament*
by Gospel Light in 1996.

Uncommon high school group study & leader's guide : the New Testament / Jim
Burns, general editor.
p. cm.
Rev. ed. of: The Word on the New Testament.
Includes bibliographical references and index.
ISBN 978-0-8307-5566-0 (trade paper : alk. paper)
1. Bible. N.T.—Study and teaching. 2. Church work with teenagers. I. Burns, Jim,
1953- II. Word on the New Testament.
BS2530.U53 2010
225.0071—dc22
2010008459

1 2 3 4 5 6 7 8 9 10 11 12 13 14 15 16 / 20 19 18 17 16 15 14 13 12 11 10

Rights for publishing this book outside the U.S.A. or in non-English languages are
administered by Gospel Light Worldwide, an international not-for-profit ministry.
For additional information, please visit www.glww.org, e-mail info@glww.org, or write
to Gospel Light Worldwide, 1957 Eastman Avenue, Ventura, CA 93003, U.S.A.

To order copies of this book and other Gospel Light products in bulk quantities,
please contact us at 1-800-446-7735.

contents

dedication

Ryan Daffron—You are one of the most gifted communicators of the gospel that I know. It is an honor to call you our pastor.

Mike DeVries—The original manuscript of this great curriculum was written by the very talented and gifted Mike DeVries. Although it has gone through some extensive changes with this edition, I want to thank you, Mike, for all your years of service in the field of youth ministry. Your impact on the lives of the kids you worked with has eternal value.

thanks and thanks again to . . .

Cindy Ward—Thank you for your help and constant faithfulness to God and to the ministry of HomeWord.

Susan Retino—Your steady work at HomeWord and your attention to detail is nothing short of a blessing.

Jim Liebelt—What a privilege to work alongside someone with your giftedness and consistency.

David Peck—You are "the man" for the HomeWord Center for Youth and Family at Azusa Pacific University. Thanks so much for all your sacrifice and extra-mile effort.

Mary Perdue—Your willingness to stick to the task of helping parents is inspiring. Thank you.

Roger Marsh—You are the most talented executive producer of any radio broadcast I know. Thanks for your sacrifice.

Ben Camp—You make things happen on the HomeWord broadcast that no one else can. Thanks for using your talents for God.

Judy Hedgren—How great that we get to work together again to change the world!

how to use the *uncommon* group bible studies

Each *Uncommon* group Bible study contains 12 sessions, which are divided into 3 stand-alone units of 4 sessions each. You may choose to teach all 12 sessions consecutively, to use just one unit, or to present individual sessions. You know your group, so do what works best for you and your students.

This is your leader's guidebook for teaching your group. Electronic files (in PDF format) of each session's student handouts are available for download at **www.gospellight.com/uncommon/the_new_testament.zip**. The handouts include the "message," "dig," "apply," "reflect" and "meditation" sections of each study and have been formatted for easy printing. You may print as many copies as you need for your group.

Each session opens with a devotional meditation written for you, the youth leader. As hectic and trying as youth work is much of the time, it's important never to neglect your interior life. Use the devotions to refocus your heart and prepare yourself to share with kids the message that has already taken root in you. Each of the 12 sessions are divided into the following sections:

starter

Young people will stay in your youth group if they feel comfortable and make friends in the group. This section is designed for you and the students to get to know each other better.

message

The message section will introduce the Scripture reading for the session and get students thinking about how the passage applies to their lives.

dig

Many young people are biblically illiterate. In this section, students will dig into the Word of God and will begin to interact on a personal level with the concepts.

apply

Young people need the opportunity to think through the issues at hand. This section will get students talking about the passage of Scripture and interacting on important issues.

reflect

The conclusion to the study will allow students to reflect on some of the issues presented in the study on a more personal level.

meditation

A closing Scripture for the students to read and reflect on.

unit I
heroes of the
new testament

Everyone needs a hero. Yet as we look around our world today, where are the heroes? Are they on television, in the movies, on the Internet? What does it take to be a hero? In a lost and searching world, our students need to see and meet more real-life heroes.

As I look in the Scriptures, I keep feeling myself drawn to the heroes. The pages of the Scriptures are filled with them: heroes who stood for what was right, heroes who stood for what was godly, heroes who had an intense love for God. These individuals, such as Peter, Paul, Timothy, Mary and scores of others, all have one thing in common: They were not heroes because they were giants of the faith, or because they were perfect, or because they had it all together. What made them heroes was that they were real and their love for God was real. They were real-life people with real-life struggles, yet they had an extraordinary love for God. Our students need to see that heroes are real people with real problems but who have an incredible love for God.

In addition to the heroes of the Bible, there stand other heroes. These individuals will never be in the pages of the Scriptures, yet I believe they are heroes in the eyes of the One who matters most. I believe that one of those heroes is you. Your students may never tell you this, but believe me, you are a hero. So to all of you who are real with students, who love them unconditionally, who choose to be transparent with your life, who love God and are willing to share that love relationship with young people: you are today's hero. When the time comes to be with Him in heaven, if any hero will get the applause of the saints and angels, I believe it will be you.

You are a hero in your work for His kingdom.

peter: failure is never final

*"Lord, if it is you," Peter replied, "tell me to come to you
on the water." "Come," he said. Then Peter got down out of the boat,
walked on the water and came toward Jesus.*

MATTHEW 14:28-29

Jesus' schedule for the day would be familiar to youth workers. After teaching all day, He proceeded to feed His hungry flock and send them home. He dismissed the disciples before He retreated to be alone with God. Personally, I would have opted for a nap or a nice quiet walk along the shore of the Galilean Sea. Instead, Jesus chose to be with the Father. Such a picture portrays the nature of Jesus Christ and unveils His motive for His mission on earth.

In the meantime, the disciples found themselves in rough waters. By the time Jesus cruised onto the scene, the fishermen feared the elements, the political zealots wished they were lobbying on dry land, and the others wanted to be anywhere else—even if it meant collecting taxes.

Jesus immediately noticed the fear of His men. He said, "Take courage. It is I. Don't be afraid" (Matthew 14:27). God will reveal Himself when we're afraid. When we face fear, frustration or futility, we need to replace our discouragement—our "dis-courage"—with the courage offered by Christ.

Peter tried to do just that. He got out of the boat and began walking on the water toward Jesus. But fast-forward a few frames in the story, and we find that Peter's courage is fleeting. He doubts. He sinks. He fails. Do you ever feel more fear than faith and more waves than wonder? Does your work with people often seem to be blown away by the wind? If so, learn from our friend Peter. Although he fears and doubts at times, Jesus labeled him "The Rock" (or "Rocky" if he were alive today).

When you find yourself in the lifeboat buffeted by the elements, follow Peter's lead. First, pray to Jesus: "Tell me to come to you." Second, listen (and wait!) for God's invitation: "Come." Don't jump overboard with your own best intentions—sometimes failure can be the result of your premature departure. Third, leave behind everything you know and trust—your confidence in your career, the comfort of the boat, the company of your friends—and go to Christ. Finally, get out and walk with Jesus, keeping your eyes on Him.

When Peter took the step of faith but then took his eyes off Jesus, he started to sink. He nearly drowned. He failed. Then he found himself face to face with the living God, who admonished him, "You of little faith, why did you doubt?" Peter's failure led him to a deeper faith and a powerful future. With Peter and the rest of us, failure is never final. Bon voyage!

Courage is resistance to fear and mastery of fear, not absence of it.
MARK TWAIN

peter: failure is never final

starter

FAILURE IS NEVER FINAL: The pages of history are filled with people who were once failures, but they are now legends. The difference between those who have led lives of excellence and those who have led lives of mediocrity lies in their willingness to fail and learn from their failures. Failure is not final; it's an opportunity to grow, learn and be used by God. Here's a look at two such people. Have a different student read each of the following portraits, and then discuss the questions as a whole group.

Portrait One: In 1978, while vacuuming his home, James Dyson realized his bag vacuum cleaner was constantly losing suction power. Dust was quickly clogging the pores of the bag and blocking the airflow so that the suction dropped rapidly. So Dyson set to work solving this problem. Five years and 5,127 prototypes later, the world's first cyclonic bagless vacuum cleaner arrived.

Dyson offered his invention to major manufacturers, but one by one they turned him down. So Dyson decided to manufacture his own vacuum cleaner. Today, with his research team, he has developed products that have achieved sales of more than $10 billion worldwide. He has used a substantial amount of this money to open the Dyson Microarray Laboratory at the Royal Marsden Hospital in London. This state-of-the-art facility helps scientists study thousands of genes at a time, identifying patterns relevant to breast cancer, its treatment and possible cure.

Although people could easily survive without Dyson's bagless vacuum cleaners, his ultimate success (after more than 5,000 prototypes) allowed Dyson to facilitate research that may eventually save millions of lives.

Portrait Two: In all the pages of history, there are few people who have failed as much as Thomas Edison. For years, Edison tried in vain to accomplish something that many said could never be done: create the light bulb! Edison made more than 900 attempts to create a light bulb before finally achieving success. More than 900 times, Edison developed a bulb only to fail and go back to the drawing board to try again. Yet in the middle of all the failure, Edison kept trying. According to Edison, every time he experienced failure he merely "found out one more way not to make a light bulb." He did not let failure become the final word for him. Eventually he did succeed, and he has since gone down in the pages of history as one of the greatest inventors of all time.

1. What would have happened if James Dyson and Thomas Edison had let failure become the final word in their lives?

    _____

    _____

    _____

    _____

2. In your opinion, what was it that kept James Dyson and Thomas Edison from giving up after they had failed so many times?

    _____

    _____

    _____

    _____

3. Why is it so easy to let failure get the best of us?

    _____

    _____

    _____

4. What are some ways to turn defeats into victories?

    _____

    _____

    _____

message

Failure is the classroom of life. Even within the pages of God's Word, failures can be seen as instruments that God used to mold and change lives. Peter is perhaps the greatest example in the New Testament of what we would consider a failure, yet God saw past his shortcomings to the potential that was within him.

Let's look at some of the important events that occurred in the life of Peter after he met Christ. In John 1:40-42 we find the story of how Jesus first called Peter and his brother, Andrew, to follow Him. As you read this passage, think about the significance of Jesus giving Peter, who was then called Simon, a new name.

Andrew, Simon Peter's brother, was one of the two who heard what John had said and who had followed Jesus. The first thing Andrew did was to find his brother Simon and tell him, "We have found the Messiah" (that is, the Christ). And he brought him to Jesus. Jesus looked at him and said, "You are Simon son of John. You will be called Cephas" (which, when translated, is Peter) (John 1:40-42).

1. Why do you think Jesus changed Simon's name to Peter?

    ----

2. What significance is there in Peter's name meaning "rock"?

    ----

3. How does it feel to know that God sees past our failures to our potential?

_____

_____

_____

_____

When Jesus first met Peter, he was an ordinary fisherman who was often brash and impulsive. After Christ entered his life, Peter didn't suddenly become perfect or stop stumbling. However, he did become a changed person with new goals and new priorities. Jesus chose Peter because he was a real person who could be changed by God's love. Often, this change came about as Peter experienced failure and received Christ's forgiveness.

Perhaps the greatest example of this occurred near the end of Jesus' time on earth. Jesus knew that He would soon be crucified, and told the disciples, "You will all fall away . . . for it is written: 'I will strike the shepherd, and the sheep will be scattered.' But after I have risen, I will go ahead of you into Galilee" (Mark 14:27-28). Peter, with the best of intentions, insisted that he would never turn away from Jesus:

> Peter declared, "Even if all fall away, I will not."
> "I tell you the truth," Jesus answered, "today—yes, tonight—before the rooster crows twice you yourself will disown me three times."
> But Peter insisted emphatically, "Even if I have to die with you, I will never disown you." And all the others said the same (Mark 14:29-31).

Skipping ahead a few verses, Jesus is arrested in the Garden of Gethsemane and is taken away to stand trial. Peter follows the procession and finds himself standing outside the courtyard where Jesus has been taken. When he is approached by a servant girl who recognizes him as a follower of Christ, we see how Peter's emphatic insistence that he would never deny Jesus plays out:

They took Jesus to the high priest, and all the chief priests, elders and teachers of the law came together. Peter followed him at a distance, right into the courtyard of the high priest. There he sat with the guards and warmed himself at the fire. . . . While Peter was below in the courtyard, one of the servant girls of the high priest came by. When she saw Peter warming himself, she looked closely at him.

"You also were with that Nazarene, Jesus," she said.

But he denied it. "I don't know or understand what you're talking about," he said, and went out into the entryway.

When the servant girl saw him there, she said again to those standing around, "This fellow is one of them." Again he denied it.

After a little while, those standing near said to Peter, "Surely you are one of them, for you are a Galilean."

He began to call down curses on himself, and he swore to them, "I don't know this man you're talking about."

Immediately the rooster crowed the second time. Then Peter remembered the word Jesus had spoken to him: "Before the rooster crows twice you will disown me three times." And he broke down and wept (Mark 14:53,66-72).

1. Why do think Peter was so confident that he would never deny Jesus?

----

2. Was there ever a time in your life when you felt that way?
    Explain.

    _____

    _____

    _____

    _____

3. What two mistakes did Peter make before he denied Jesus
    (see Mark 14:30,38)?

    _____

    _____

    _____

    _____

4. God knows our weaknesses. Is that a comfort or a burden
    to you? Why?

    _____

    _____

    _____

    _____

dig

Peter denied Christ three times, just as Jesus said he would. But
that was not the end of the story for Peter. After Jesus was laid to
rest in the tomb on a Friday, early the next Sunday morning,
three women (named Mary, Salome and Mary Magdalene) went
to the tomb to anoint Jesus' body with spices (which was the cus-
tom of the time). When they entered the tomb, instead of finding
the body of Jesus, they encountered a man wearing a white robe.
The man said to them:

Don't be alarmed. . . . You are looking for Jesus the Nazarene, who was crucified. He has risen! He is not here. See the place where they laid him. But go; tell his disciples and Peter, "He is going ahead of you into Galilee. There you will see him, just as he told you" (Mark 16:6-7).

1. What was the significance of the angel's words "and Peter"?

   _____

   _____

   _____

   _____

   _____

2. How do you think Peter felt when he heard that the angel had said this?

   _____

   _____

   _____

   _____

   _____

The book of Luke tells us that when Peter heard what the women said, he "got up and ran to the tomb. Bending over, he saw the strips of linen lying by themselves, and he went away, wondering to himself what had happened" (Luke 24:12). Peter was trying to make sense of it all.

Later, the resurrected Jesus appeared to seven of the disciples, including Peter, by the Sea of Tiberias. The men had been fishing all night, but had nothing to show for it. Suddenly, a man called to them from the shore about 100 yards from the boat and instructed them to cast their nets on the other side of the boat. They did so and caught so many fish that they couldn't even pull up the net. When Peter realized the man instructing them from the shore was Jesus, he jumped into the water and swam to Him. Once the other six disciples reached the shore, Jesus shared breakfast with them. John 21:15-19 tells the conclusion of the story:

When they had finished eating, Jesus said to Simon Peter, "Simon son of John, do you truly love me more than these?"

"Yes, Lord," he said, "you know that I love you."

Jesus said, "Feed my lambs." Again Jesus said, "Simon son of John, do you truly love me?"

He answered, "Yes, Lord, you know that I love you."

Jesus said, "Take care of my sheep." The third time he said to him, "Simon son of John, do you love me?"

Peter was hurt because Jesus asked him the third time, "Do you love me?" He said, "Lord, you know all things; you know that I love you."

Jesus said, "Feed my sheep. I tell you the truth, when you were younger you dressed yourself and went where you wanted; but when you are old you will stretch out your hands, and someone else will dress you and lead you where you do not want to go." Jesus said this to indicate the kind of death by which Peter would glorify God. Then he said to him, "Follow me!"

1. If you were Peter, how would you have felt standing before Jesus as He asked you, "Do you love me"?

   _____

   _____

   _____

   _____

   _____

2. How would you have felt standing before Christ as He restored you and said, "Follow Me"?

   _____

   _____

   _____

   _____

   _____

3. Why do you think Peter jumped into the water and swam
   to shore when he realized it was Jesus?

   _____

   _____

   _____

   _____

4. Why did Jesus ask Peter three times if he loved Him? What
   purpose did Jesus have in restoring Peter into a right relationship with Him in front of the other disciples?

   _____

   _____

   _____

   _____

   _____

5. How does it make you feel to know that God sees beyond
   your failures and can forgive and restore you? Explain.

   _____

   _____

   _____

   _____

During Jesus' ministry, Peter had been a bit of an unstable leader with a defiant swagger. Christ had now forgiven him and restored him. When Jesus was preparing to leave the earth after His resurrection, He told the disciples, "Do not leave Jerusalem, but wait for the gift my Father promised, which you have heard me speak about. . . . You will receive power when the Holy Spirit comes on you; and you will be my witnesses in Jerusalem, and in all Judea and Samaria, and to the ends of the earth" (Acts 1:4,8).

Peter and the disciples followed what Jesus had said and waited in an upper room in Jerusalem. Then, on the Day of Pentecost, a sound like the rushing of a violent wind came from heaven and filled the whole house. All of them were filled with the Holy Spirit and began to speak in other languages. When the crowd heard them, some thought that the believers were drunk. In response, Peter, through the power of the Holy Spirit, stood up and began to address the people.

> *"Men of Israel, listen to this: Jesus of Nazareth was a man accredited by God to you by miracles, wonders and signs, which God did among you through him, as you yourselves know. This man was handed over to you by God's set purpose and foreknowledge; and you, with the help of wicked men, put him to death by nailing him to the cross. But God raised him from the dead, freeing him from the agony of death, because it was impossible for death to keep its hold on him. . . . Therefore let all Israel be assured of this: God has made this Jesus, whom you crucified, both Lord and Christ."*
>
> *When the people heard this, they were cut to the heart and said to Peter and the other apostles, "Brothers, what shall we do?"*
>
> *Peter replied, "Repent and be baptized, every one of you, in the name of Jesus Christ for the forgiveness of your sins. And you will receive the gift of the Holy Spirit. The promise is for you and*

your children and for all who are far off—for all whom the Lord our God will call."

With many other words he warned them; and he pleaded with them, "Save yourselves from this corrupt generation." Those who accepted his message were baptized, and about three thousand were added to their number that day (Acts 2:22-24,36-41).

1. How did God use Peter?

     _____

     _____

     _____

     _____

2. What were the results of Peter's obedience?

     _____

     _____

     _____

3. Even though Peter felt like a failure, God used him as a part of His plan to touch lives. What hope can be found for you personally from these verses in Acts?

     _____

     _____

     _____

     _____

God went on to use Peter in many miraculous ways. He was beaten and thrown in prison on several occasions, but he never again denied that he knew Christ or tried to distance himself from the

Lord. Peter became one of the main leaders in the Early Church—a true "rock" and foundation of the growing community, just as Jesus had said.

apply

1. Peter denied Jesus out of fear and pride. We are all like Peter because we are all guilty of denying Christ as Lord in particular areas of our lives. What is one area of your life in which you need to make Jesus the Lord?

2. As we look at Peter's mistakes, what are two practices that you can apply to your life to help you accomplish this?

3. In what areas does God want to use you?

4. Are you truly willing to keep following Jesus, even when you fail? If so, how will you persevere?

_____

_____

_____

_____

5. Jesus changed Simon's name to "The Rock." If you allowed Jesus to intently look at you, to what would He change your name? Why?

_____

_____

_____

_____

reflect

1. How does it feel to know that . . .

    God knows your potential?

    _____

    _____

    _____

    _____

    God knows your weaknesses and failures?

    _____

    _____

    _____

    _____

God is in the business of restoration?

_____

_____

_____

_____

God wants to use you?

_____

_____

_____

_____

2. What are some areas of your life where failure has turned out to be an opportunity?

    _____

    _____

    _____

    _____

3. Why is it often so difficult to see past our weaknesses and failures to the potential God sees in us?

    _____

    _____

    _____

    _____

4. In 2 Corinthians 12:9-10, Paul writes, "I will boast all the more gladly about my weaknesses, so that Christ's power may rest on me. That is why, for Christ's sake, I delight in weaknesses, in insults, in hardships, in persecutions, in difficulties. For when I am weak, then I am strong." How

does this passage relate to what you've learned about Peter? How does it relate to your own life?

_____

_____

_____

_____

5. How does it make you feel to know that God's power can be displayed in our weaknesses?

_____

_____

_____

_____

6. What action step will you take to apply what you have learned in this session about yourself?

_____

_____

_____

_____

_____

meditation

And the God of all grace, who called you to eternal glory
in Christ, after you have suffered a little while, will himself
restore you and make you strong, firm and steadfast.

1 Peter 5:10

paul: having a heart for others

*Fourteen years later I went up again to Jerusalem, this time
with Barnabas. I took Titus along also.*

GALATIANS 2:1

Barnabas was a partner with Paul, while Titus was a disciple of
Paul's. Both men spent much time with Paul as they worked together to further the gospel of Christ. A striking aspect of Paul's
ministry is not only his preaching of love to others—"Love is patient, love is kind . . . love never fails" (1 Corinthians 13:4,8)—but
also the proof of his love. Paul's commitment to Christ com-
pelled him to be compassionate. Both his words and his ways revealed his heart for others. If you want to know a person's heart,
don't just listen, but also watch.

Youth ministry, as modeled by the ministry of Paul, is a business of "going with" and "taking along also." Barnabas was the

man whom Paul was "going with." Barnabas was a landowner who valued God's work more than his own worth (see Acts 4:36). He donated his money, his time and his heart to God's work in partnership with Paul.

Who is your Barnabas? Who is your peer with whom you share your vision, your needs, your pain and your joys? My personal experience shows that the finest relationships I have developed in my years of ministry came from the people with whom I shared ministry. Paul had a heart for others, and Barnabas was blessed by Paul's heart.

Youth ministry is a task of "taking along also." Titus was a younger disciple of Paul's; a man Paul refers to with these kind-hearted words: "Titus, my true son, in our common faith" (Titus 1:4). Like a father to his son, Paul revealed his heart to Titus as they ministered together. Later, Paul left Titus behind in Crete to lead a ministry. There is no greater encouragement to a minister than to see your heart for Christ duplicated in your own disciples.

Who is your Titus? With whom can you not only share the words of a teaching curriculum but your very heart? Next time you are going to minister somewhere, ask yourself, *Who can go with me as a partner?* or *Who can I also take with me as a disciple?* You may find a ministry more powerful, enjoyable and rewarding than you ever imagined. Remember that when two or three are gathered together in Christ's name, the King is in their midst (see Matthew 18:20).

The glory of friendship is not the outstretched hand, nor the
kindly smile, nor the joy of companionship; it's the spiritual inspiration
that comes to one when he discovers that someone else believes in
him and is willing to trust him with his friendship.

RALPH WALDO EMERSON

group study guide

paul: having a heart for others

starter

WHO SUPPORTS YOU? Divide the students into groups of three or four. Have each group read the descriptions that follow and then write the name of a person in their lives who best fits the description given. Have them try to use a different person for each description, and then ask them to share their answers with the other members of their small groups. Ask them to identify what role they find themselves playing the most, and what role they think they should play more often.

_____ The Rock: solid in times of crisis
_____ The Peacemaker: has the gift of diffusing conflict

Note: You can download this group study guide in 8¹/₂" x 11" format at **www.gospellight.com/uncommon/the_new_testament.zip.**

_____ The Encourager: brings a smile to your face when you are down

_____ The Sage: full of wise words and good advice

_____ Old Faithful: has been there with you through thick and thin

_____ Comforter: helps you get through the sad times in life

1. What role do you find yourself playing the most? Why?

_____
_____
_____
_____

2. What role do you need to play more? Why

_____
_____
_____
_____

message

Saul was raised an orthodox Jew and grew up to be a rabbi, a teacher and even a Pharisee. He started out as an enemy of Christ, having Jesus' followers arrested and taking pleasure in their deaths. But God intervened in Saul's life and got a hold of his heart. His name was changed to Paul, and he spent his years pouring out his life for the sake of his Savior. Paul's life was marked by an incredible heart for helping and encouraging others. From Jerusalem, to Syria, to Asia, to Macedonia and all the way to Rome,

Paul took care of the needs of others. His passion was to see people changed by the incredible love of God. He acted justly and loved mercy. God is calling us to that same mission of caring for, sharing with and encouraging others.

caring for others

When Paul lived among the Thessalonians, he did not coerce them, seek their praises or financially burden them as he taught the gospel to them. Although he was entitled to receive financial support from the people, he supported himself as a tentmaker. He focused his efforts on purely and honestly presenting God's message of salvation to the people. In 1 Thessalonians 2:1-9, Paul shares how he had ministered to them:

> *You know, brothers, that our visit to you was not a failure. We had previously suffered and been insulted in Philippi, as you know, but with the help of our God we dared to tell you his gospel in spite of strong opposition. For the appeal we make does not spring from error or impure motives, nor are we trying to trick you. On the contrary, we speak as men approved by God to be entrusted with the gospel. We are not trying to please men but God, who tests our hearts. You know we never used flattery, nor did we put on a mask to cover up greed—God is our witness. We were not looking for praise from men, not from you or anyone else.*
>
> *As apostles of Christ we could have been a burden to you, but we were gentle among you, like a mother caring for her little children. We loved you so much that we were delighted to share with you not only the gospel of God but our lives as well, because you had become so dear to us. Surely you remember, brothers, our toil and hardship; we worked night and day in order not to be a burden to anyone while we preached the gospel of God to you.*

1. What motivation did Paul give for why he wanted to share
    the gospel with the Thessalonians?

    _____

    _____

    _____

    _____

2. What characteristics did Paul demonstrate that showed
    he had a caring heart?

    _____

    _____

    _____

    _____

3. How does Paul describe the way in which he treated the
    Thessalonians?

    _____

    _____

    _____

    _____

4. Why was it important for Paul to stress that he and the
    other apostles had not been a burden on them?

    _____

    _____

    _____

    _____

sharing with others

Paul went on three separate missionary journeys, preaching the gospel of Christ throughout the known world at that time. His whole purpose in life was to speak out boldly for Christ and to become more like Him. He surrendered his life to the leadership of the Holy Spirit and openly shared his life with others, hoping that his example would lead them closer to Christ. In 1 Corinthians 2:1-5 and 1 Timothy 1:15-16, he humbly explains his motives:

> *When I came to you, brothers, I did not come with eloquence or superior wisdom as I proclaimed to you the testimony about God. For I resolved to know nothing while I was with you except Jesus Christ and him crucified. I came to you in weakness and fear, and with much trembling. My message and my preaching were not with wise and persuasive words, but with a demonstration of the Spirit's power, so that your faith might not rest on men's wisdom, but on God's power* (1 Corinthians 2:1-5).

> *Christ Jesus came into the world to save sinners—of whom I am the worst. But for that very reason I was shown mercy so that in me, the worst of sinners, Christ Jesus might display his unlimited patience as an example for those who would believe on him and receive eternal life* (1 Timothy 1:16).

1. How does Paul describe the way in which he brought the gospel to the Corinthian believers?

    ----

2. What does this tell us about the importance of relying on the power and influence of God when sharing the gospel?

_____

_____

_____

_____

3. What was Paul's singular focus while he was among the Corinthians?

_____

_____

_____

_____

4. By his own admission, Paul was "the worst of sinners." How did this enable him to have compassion on others and share the gospel with them?

_____

_____

_____

_____

5. How does sharing the gospel and sharing our lives go hand in hand?

_____

_____

_____

_____

dig

Barnabas came alongside Paul and encouraged him in his ministry. In Acts 9:26-27, we read how Barnabas had the ability to see into Paul's heart and encourage him:

When he [Paul] came to Jerusalem, he tried to join the disciples, but they were all afraid of him, not believing that he really was a disciple. But Barnabas took him and brought him to the apostles.

Beth Moore describes Barnabas this way: "Barnabas offers us an example we don't want to miss. His name had been Joseph, but the disciples renamed him 'son of encouragement.' Barnabas persuaded the apostles to accept the new convert, and the most powerful preacher in all Christendom was set loose in Jerusalem. God used Barnabas over and over to give others the courage to be the people He called them to be."[1]

God sees incredible potential in everyone. Part of the job of encouragers is to help others see what God sees in them and live out that potential in their lives. In 1 Thessalonians 2:11-12, Paul describes how he encouraged the Thessalonian believers:

For you know that we dealt with each of you as a father deals with his own children, encouraging, comforting and urging you to live lives worthy of God, who calls you into his kingdom and glory.

1. Who has encouraged you lately? In what way has that person encouraged you?

    ----

2. How does encouragement affect . . .

    Your view of yourself?

    _____

    _____

    _____

    _____

    Your view of God?

    _____

    _____

    _____

    _____

    Your spiritual growth?

    _____

    _____

    _____

    _____

3. What keeps you from encouraging others more often?

    _____

    _____

    _____

    _____

    _____

4. What was one time when you felt the most encouraged by someone?

_____

_____

_____

_____

_____

5. What was one time when you felt that God used you as a source of encouragement in another person's life?

_____

_____

_____

_____

_____

6. What are some practical ways that you can encourage others in their relationships with God?

_____

_____

_____

_____

_____

7. What can you do this week to be more of a servant to those in your family?

_____

_____

_____

_____

_____

8. What can you do this week to have more of a servant's heart for those outside of your family?

_____

_____

_____

_____

apply

In a real sense, we are the hands, feet and voice of Jesus in this world. When we reach out to others with a heart of deep concern, lives are changed as a result. Paul understood this, and his life was one that was marked by a deep concern for others. In Philippians 2:1-4, he writes:

> If you have any encouragement from being united with Christ, if any comfort from his love, if any fellowship with the Spirit, if any tenderness and compassion, then make my joy complete by being like-minded, having the same love, being one in spirit and purpose. Do nothing out of selfish ambition or vain conceit, but in humility consider others better than yourselves. Each of you should look not only to your own interests, but also to the interests of others.

1. Who is one person in your life who needs to feel cared for? What specific action can you take to care for that person?

Person:

_____

_____

_____

_____

Action:

_____

_____

_____

_____

2. Who in your life needs to hear about the gospel of God?
   What action can you take to share Jesus with that person?

Person:

_____

_____

_____

_____

Action:

_____

_____

_____

_____

3. Who in your life needs to be encouraged? What practical
   steps can you take to encourage that person this week?

Person:

_____

_____

_____

Action:

_____

_____

_____

_____

4. Who is the most "others-centered" person that you know? What is it about that person that makes you think of him or her that way?

Person:

_____

_____

_____

_____

Why he or she is others-centered:

_____

_____

_____

_____

5. What do the following verses say about having a heart for others?

Galatians 6:2

_____

_____

_____

_____

_____

Philippians 2:1-4

_____

_____

_____

_____

1 Thessalonians 2:8,12

_____

_____

_____

_____

Hebrews 10:24-25

_____

_____

_____

_____

reflect

1. Which of the three areas—caring, sharing or encouraging—do you need to work on the most?

_____

_____

_____

_____

2. Why do you think you hold back in this area?

_____

_____

_____

_____

3. What will it require of you to grow in this area?

_____

_____

_____

_____

4. Do you think the reward for growing in this area will outweigh the risk? Why or why not?

_____

_____

_____

_____

meditation

Be devoted to one another in brotherly love.
Honor one another above yourselves. Never be lacking in
zeal, but keep your spiritual fervor, serving the Lord.
Be joyful in hope, patient in affliction, faithful in prayer.
Share with God's people who are in need.

ROMANS 12:10-12

Note

1. Beth Moore, *To Live Is Christ, Joining Paul's Journey of Faith* (Nashville, TN: B&H Publishing Group, 2001), pp. 50-51.

session 3

timothy: a worthy example

And the things you have heard me say in the presence of many witnesses entrust to reliable men who will also be qualified to teach others.

2 TIMOTHY 2:2

"Sure, I'll do that in the morning." The words came ringing back to Doug as he heard the water running. The previous night, his wife had asked him if he would reprogram the sprinkler system to run three times a day instead of just once. The family had just gotten a new dog, Molly, and every time the dog showed up in the yard, she left a few new "burn" spots in the grass. The family has just reseeded the lawn to cover the spots, which required more frequent watering. Doug had forgotten all about setting the sprinkler system, and now he knew that he was in the "Doughouse."

As Doug remembered the promise he had made to his wife, he realized that more often than not, her concern had less to do with the dog showing up and more to do with *him* not showing up. He knew that whenever he promised something but failed to deliver on it, it left a burn mark on his integrity. Granted, in this case his wife would likely offer him forgiveness as he shuffled downstairs with his tail between his legs, groveling at her feet as he begged for mercy. She would reach into "Doug's emotional bowl" and pull out stored up reliability to cover for his "oops." However, if he continued to promise and not deliver, he knew that his family would be left with the perpetual task of covering Dad's spots.

All of us can relate in some way to Doug's situation. When we make a promise, we place hope in the form of an expectation in the hearts of others. When that promise fizzles, the expectation is dashed. An emotional withdrawal is taken from their heart, and unless they have an abundance of emotional deposits, they will quickly find themselves overdrawn. Beyond the relational deficit, something else happens: we lose our integrity. That absence of integrity causes feelings of hopelessness in others.

The power of the promise kept is the crux of the gospel. Jesus told us ahead of time that He would pay the price for our sins, and He came through the death and resurrection as He promised. Likewise, Paul knew that when he entrusted his commands to Timothy, young Tim would deliver.

Tim was a man of integrity. People with integrity gain trust from their leaders and let them know that they will carry through on the task. People with integrity offer promises. People who promise offer hope. People who deliver on that promise fulfill hope and build integrity. People with integrity, like Timothy, gain the trust and get the commission from God.

The reputation of a thousand years may be determined
by the conduct of one hour.
JAPANESE PROVERB

timothy: a worthy example

starter

IF I: Have students complete as many of the following statements as possible in five minutes. When the time has concluded, have them share responses from at least one of their statements.

1. If I won the lottery, I would . . .

    _____
    _____
    _____

2. If I could travel anywhere, I would go . . .

    _____
    _____
    _____
    _____

3. If I could be anyone in the world, I would be like . . .

    _____

    _____

    _____

4. If I could have any job in the world, I would be . . .

    _____

    _____

    _____

5. If I had a month to live, I would . . .

    _____

    _____

    _____

    _____

6. If I had the power to go back in time, I would . . .

    _____

    _____

    _____

    _____

message

Most of what we know about Timothy comes from a few passages in the book of Acts, the two letters written to him by Paul, and a few other references to him in Paul's other letters. In Acts 16, Timothy first appears on the scene when Paul and Silas arrive at the town of Lystra, where Timothy lived. His mother, Eunice, and grandmother, Lois, were both believers in Christ, and they had set an example of a godly life for Timothy since he was young. Paul wanted to take Timothy with him on his journey, and he ultimately became one of Paul's close traveling companions.

Timothy was faithful to the work that had been set before him and impressed Paul with his dedication. In his letter to the Philippians, Paul wrote, "I have no one else like him, who takes a genuine interest in your welfare . . . Timothy has proved himself, because as a son with his father he has served with me in the work of the gospel" (Philippians 2:20,22).

Later, when Timothy became the pastor of a church in Ephesus, Paul wrote a series of letters to him to advise him on some of the practical matters of leading a congregation. One of the areas that Paul stressed to the young Timothy was that it was important for him to set a good example of what living a godly life should look like. Paul knew that the way in which a person leads his or her life would influence others—whether positively or negatively—on how they viewed God. In 1 Timothy 4:12, he challenged Timothy to set an example to his congregation in five specific areas: "Set an example for the believers in *speech*, in *life*, in *love*, in *faith* and in *purity*" (emphasis added).

Today, we will take a closer look at each of these five areas and see how they apply to our particular situations.

speech

The first area in which Paul challenged Timothy was in his speech. In Paul's letter to the Ephesians, he explains how speech can be used as a tool to draw people closer to Christ:

> *Do not let any unwholesome talk come out of your mouths, but only what is helpful for building others up according to their needs, that it may benefit those who listen* (Ephesians 4:29).

1. What do you think Paul meant by "unwholesome talk"?

   ----

2. Why is it important to only say that which is helpful to others?

   ----

life

The second area in which Paul challenged Timothy to be an example was in the way he lived his life. In his letters to the Ephesians and the Thessalonians, Paul described several ways in which people can lead a godly life:

> As a prisoner for the Lord, then, I urge you to live a life worthy of the calling you have received. Be completely humble and gentle; be patient, bearing with one another in love. Make every effort to keep the unity of the Spirit through the bond of peace. There is one body and one Spirit—just as you were called to one hope when you were called—one Lord, one faith, one baptism; one God and Father of all, who is over all and through all and in all (Ephesians 4:1-6).

> You are witnesses, and so is God, of how holy, righteous and blameless we were among you who believed. For you know that we dealt with each of you as a father deals with his own children, encouraging, comforting and urging you to live lives worthy of God, who calls you into his kingdom and glory (1 Thessalonians 2:10-12).

1. What do you think it means to "live a life worthy of the calling you have received"?

    _____

    _____

    _____

2. What did Paul tell the Ephesians were the characteristics of such a life?

    _____

    _____

    _____

    _____

love

The third way in which Paul challenged Timothy to be an example was in the way he demonstrated God's love to others. There are many things in our culture that people label "love," but in 1 John, the apostle gives a detailed description of what godly love should really look like:

> *This is how we know what love is: Jesus Christ laid down his life for us. And we ought to lay down our lives for our brothers. If anyone has material possessions and sees his brother in need but has no pity on him, how can the love of God be in him? Dear children, let us not love with words or tongue but with actions and in truth. . . .*
>
> *Dear friends, let us love one another, for love comes from God. Everyone who loves has been born of God and knows God. Whoever does not love does not know God, because God is love. This is how God showed his love among us: He sent his one and only Son into the world that we might live through him. This is love: not that we loved God, but that he loved us and sent his Son as an atoning*

sacrifice for our sins. Dear friends, since God so loved us, we also ought to love one another. No one has ever seen God; but if we love one another, God lives in us and his love is made complete in us (1 John 3:16-18; 4:7-12).

1. How does John say that we will know what love is? What does this mean to you?

_____

_____

_____

_____

2. What actions will we take if we truly love others?

_____

_____

_____

_____

3. What do these verses say loving others will reveal about our relationship with God?

_____

_____

_____

_____

faith

The fourth way in which Paul challenged Timothy to be an example was in the way he demonstrated his faith to others. Faith means placing one's trust, future and hope in God, knowing that His character is certain and His Word is reliable. The author of Hebrews states the following about faith:

Now faith is being sure of what we hope for and certain of what we do not see. This is what the ancients were commended for. By faith we understand that the universe was formed at God's command, so that what is seen was not made out of what was visible (Hebrews 11:1-3).

Paul described his journey of faith to Timothy as taking part in a race in which he was pursuing a singular goal:

For I am already being poured out like a drink offering, and the time has come for my departure. I have fought the good fight, I have finished the race, I have kept the faith. Now there is in store for me the crown of righteousness, which the Lord, the righteous Judge, will award to me on that day—and not only to me, but also to all who have longed for his appearing (2 Timothy 4:6-8).

1. What did Paul mean when he said that he had "fought the good fight"?

    _____

    _____

    _____

    _____

    _____

2. What was the reward that Paul knew was in store for him for keeping the faith?

    _____

    _____

    _____

    _____

    _____

3. What does Paul say to Timothy about what lies is store for those who follow his example?

    _____

    _____

    _____

    _____

purity

The final area in which Paul advised Timothy to set a good example was in purity. Purity applies to all areas of life—to a person's outer body as well as his or her inner self. Paul had the following advice for the Corinthian believers on keeping pure:

> *Flee from sexual immorality. All other sins a man commits are outside his body, but he who sins sexually sins against his own body. Do you not know that your body is a temple of the Holy Spirit, who is in you, whom you have received from God? You are not your own; you were bought at a price. Therefore honor God with your body* (1 Corinthians 6:18-20).

The apostle Peter had this to say on the subject:

> *Your beauty should not come from outward adornment, such as braided hair and the wearing of gold jewelry and fine clothes. Instead, it should be that of your inner self, the unfading beauty of a gentle and quiet spirit, which is of great worth in God's sight* (1 Peter 3:3-4).

1. In what way is our body a temple of the Holy Spirit?

    _____

    _____

    _____

2. According to the apostle Peter, where should our true
    beauty come from?

    _____

    _____

    _____

    _____

3. Why would keeping pure help a young leader like Timo-
    thy? What kind of example would he set?

    _____

    _____

    _____

dig

1. How do our words affect our example of how we live out
    our faith?

    _____

    _____

    _____

    _____

2. In the following table, give some examples of destructive
    words and some examples of constructive words.

Destructive Words	Constructive Words

3. In what ways should our lifestyles be different because we are followers of Jesus Christ?

4. Think about the type of godly love that John describes in 1 John 3:16-18 and 4:7-12. What keeps us from loving others with that same type of love?

5. How would leading a lifestyle of love have an impact on those around us?

6. What are some practical ways to keep your faith and strengthen it?

apply

As we can see from the life of Timothy, one of the greatest ways that we can impact the world and those around us is by living a godly life. Through our example, we can make the gospel attractive to others and compel them to want to know Christ. When others see us live out our faith every day, it brings credibility to the gospel.

So, how are you doing in the way you speak, live your life, love as God loves, share your faith and maintain your purity? Take a few minutes and do the following integrity inventory. Complete the inventory using a scale of 1 to 10, with 1 meaning that you generally disagree/need some help in this area and 10 meaning that you generally agree/are doing great.

speech
_____ My words are marked by honesty.
_____ The words that I say build others up.
_____ When I make a promise, I keep it.
_____ My comments to others are constructive, not destructive.

life
_____ What I believe impacts how I live my life.
_____ I seek to live a life of integrity.
_____ I regularly consider how my life reflects what I believe and what I say.
_____ The way I lead my life around my family shows that I am a follower of Christ.

love
_____ I seek to see others through the eyes of Jesus Christ.
_____ I seek to love others unselfishly with my actions and not just my words.

_____ I am currently involved in some action that is expressing my love for others.

_____ The way I love others reflects the way in which I feel God loves me.

faith

_____ I sense a deepening of my faith and love relationship with Christ.

_____ I do activities that help deepen my faith and relationship with Christ.

_____ I seek ways to share my faith with others.

_____ I always try to demonstrate my faith when I am around my family and others.

purity

_____ I seem to have a pure heart before God.

_____ The things that I put into my mind, heart and soul encourage purity.

_____ I desire to honor God with my body.

_____ I lead a life of purity around my family and others.

Add up your scores in each of the five areas and list these totals in the space below:

Speech: _____   Faith: _____

Life: _____   Purity: _____

Love: _____

Now check your scores!

4 to 7   You need to do some work in this area!

8 to 12   Could use some improvement in this area.

13 to 16   You are doing pretty well in this area.
17 to 20   You have no real problems in this area.

List the main areas in which you are doing well and those areas
you need to work on. What will you do to grow in each area?

_____

_____

_____

_____

reflect

1.   How can you set a better example in the words you speak?

_____

_____

_____

_____

2.   What are some areas you need to examine in your life as
     an issue of integrity?

_____

_____

_____

_____

3.   What can you do to be more actively involved in loving
     others?

_____

_____

_____

_____

4. What can you do to better promote purity within your sphere of influence?

    _____

    _____

    _____

    _____

    _____

5. What are some of the struggles you might have in keeping your faith?

    _____

    _____

    _____

    _____

    _____

6. What impact would living a more godly life have on your relationship with God, your family and others?

    _____

    _____

    _____

    _____

    _____

meditation

Blessed are the pure in heart for they will see God.

MATTHEW 5:8

mary: ordinary person, extraordinary faith

On the third day a wedding took place at Cana in Galilee. Jesus' mother was there. . . . When the wine was gone, Jesus' mother said to him, "They have no more wine." . . . His mother said to the servants, "Do whatever he tells you."

JOHN 2:1,3,5

Mary is a hero for believers today. Who was this woman who was chosen to be the earthly mother of the Son of God? There are two important aspects to Mary's position in Scripture: (1) she was the mother of Jesus, and (2) she was an example of faith.

Being a mother means that a woman must spend nine months watching her body bloat to what she considers astronomic proportions. After the gestation period (sounds like an intestinal condition, doesn't it?), she then must endure life's most excruciating pain as she delivers an infant with a huge head who travels through a small opening in a short amount of time. From that joy-filled, pain-packed moment forward, a mom's job is to lose her job. She raises her children in such a way that they will one day be responsible adults who will no longer need her day-to-day guidance.

Mary was such a mom who knew that she was raising a child to be an adult. She is an example of faith because she believed God and obediently raised His Son. In Mary's case, she not only knew that she would one day have to release her child like every mother must do, but also that she would watch Him suffer unbearably. The prophet Simeon warned Mary that people would speak and act violently against Jesus and that, for her, it would be like a sword piercing her soul (see Luke 2:34-35). Many mothers fear such cruel treatment of their child. Few, if any, receive such a clear and accurate prophecy that it will occur.

What was behind Mary's faith? She knew and believed God. Her Son was who God said He was—the promised Messiah. We see how this affected her life in the story of the wedding at Cana (see John 2:1-11). When a problem came up and the wine ran dry, Mary—a picture of faith—went to her Son and told Him of the need: "They have no more wine." After Mary made this request, she exhibited the next great step of faith. She commissioned the servants to do whatever Jesus told them to do.

A person of faith—whether a mom, dad or youth worker trying to help moms and dads get their children through adolescence— needs to emulate Mary. Take your need to Jesus, and then do whatever Jesus tells you to do. Letting go and believing is a heroic act. Many moms manifest such heroic faith on a daily basis.

To nourish children and raise them against odds is in any time, any place, more valuable than to fix bolts in cars or design nuclear weapons.

A FRENCH PROVERB

mary: ordinary person, extraordinary faith

starter

STEPPING OUT IN FAITH: Divide students into pairs. Have one of the partners close his or her eyes while the other partner leads him or her around the inside or outside of the building. (Caution: make sure that you tell those who do the leading that they are responsible for their "blind" person's safety!) Give each pair about three minutes for the first person to lead the other. After three minutes, have the partners switch roles. When the six minutes are up, gather the entire group together and discuss the following questions:

Note: You can download this group study guide in 8½" x 11" format at www.gospellight.com/uncommon/the_new_testament.zip.

1. How did you feel while being led around?

    _____

    _____

    _____

    _____

2. Was it difficult for you to keep your eyes closed and trust
    your partner? Why or why not?

    _____

    _____

    _____

    _____

3. Could you trust the person leading you around? Why or
    why not?

    _____

    _____

    _____

    _____

4. How does this exercise relate to trusting God and having
    faith in Him?

    _____

    _____

    _____

    _____

message

In all of the New Testament, one of the greatest portraits of faith is
Mary. Mary had an incredible faith and trust in God—in what He

said and what He wanted to do through her. She took God at His word, was favored by Him, was a faithful follower of His law and was thoughtful, obedient, believing, worshipful and teachable. God's desire is the same for us: He wants us to be people of faith.

the angel's announcement to mary

We catch a glimpse of Mary's character in the story of the birth of Christ told in the Gospel of Luke. Read the following passage in Luke 1:26-56:

> *In the sixth month, God sent the angel Gabriel to Nazareth, a town in Galilee, to a virgin pledged to be married to a man named Joseph, a descendant of David. The virgin's name was Mary. The angel went to her and said, "Greetings, you who are highly favored! The Lord is with you."*
>
> *Mary was greatly troubled at his words and wondered what kind of greeting this might be. But the angel said to her, "Do not be afraid, Mary, you have found favor with God. You will be with child and give birth to a son, and you are to give him the name Jesus. He will be great and will be called the Son of the Most High. The Lord God will give him the throne of his father David, and he will reign over the house of Jacob forever; his kingdom will never end."*
>
> *"How will this be," Mary asked the angel, "since I am a virgin?"*
>
> *The angel answered, "The Holy Spirit will come upon you, and the power of the Most High will overshadow you. So the holy one to be born will be called the Son of God. Even Elizabeth your relative is going to have a child in her old age, and she who was said to be barren is in her sixth month. For nothing is impossible with God."*
>
> *"I am the Lord's servant," Mary answered. "May it be to me as you have said." Then the angel left her.*

At that time Mary got ready and hurried to a town in the hill country of Judea, where she entered Zechariah's home and greeted Elizabeth. When Elizabeth heard Mary's greeting, the baby leaped in her womb, and Elizabeth was filled with the Holy Spirit. In a loud voice she exclaimed: "Blessed are you among women, and blessed is the child you will bear! But why am I so favored, that the mother of my Lord should come to me? As soon as the sound of your greeting reached my ears, the baby in my womb leaped for joy. Blessed is she who has believed that what the Lord has said to her will be accomplished!"

And Mary said: "My soul glorifies the Lord and my spirit rejoices in God my Savior, for he has been mindful of the humble state of his servant. From now on all generations will call me blessed, for the Mighty One has done great things for me—holy is his name. His mercy extends to those who fear him, from generation to generation. He has performed mighty deeds with his arm; he has scattered those who are proud in their inmost thoughts. He has brought down rulers from their thrones but has lifted up the humble. He has filled the hungry with good things but has sent the rich away empty. He has helped his servant Israel, remembering to be merciful to Abraham and his descendants forever, even as he said to our fathers."

Mary stayed with Elizabeth for about three months and then returned home.

1. How did the angel greet Mary to tell her the news?

---

2. How did Mary react to the angel's announcement?

_____

_____

_____

3. What were Mary's initial doubts?

_____

_____

_____

4. In addition to announcing the news that she would give birth to the Messiah, what else did the angel tell Mary?

_____

_____

_____

5. How did Elizabeth greet Mary? In what ways was this similar to the angel's greeting?

_____

_____

_____

6. How did Mary respond? What does her response tell you about her relationship with the Lord?

_____

_____

_____

the angel's announcement to joseph

To understand the depth of Mary's faith, it is important to look at her specific situation at the time of the announcement. Mary was betrothed to a man named Joseph. In the ancient world, "betrothal" was the first part of a two-stage marriage process. The initial phase, the betrothal, involved a formal, witnessed agreement to marry and the giving of a bridal price (see Malachi 2:14). At this point, the bride legally became the groom's and could be called his wife. The actual marriage followed about a year later, and it was at this point that the husband took his wife home. Gabriel broke the news to Mary that she would be giving birth to the Savior during this betrothal stage, as the following passage from Matthew 1:18-25 relates:

> *This is how the birth of Jesus Christ came about: His mother Mary was pledged to be married to Joseph, but before they came together, she was found to be with child through the Holy Spirit. Because Joseph her husband was a righteous man and did not want to expose her to public disgrace, he had in mind to divorce her quietly. But after he had considered this, an angel of the Lord appeared to him in a dream and said, "Joseph son of David, do not be afraid to take Mary home as your wife, because what is conceived in her is from the Holy Spirit. She will give birth to a son, and you are to give him the name Jesus, because he will save his people from their sins." All this took place to fulfill what the Lord had said through the prophet: "The virgin will be with child and will give birth to a son, and they will call him Immanuel"—which means, "God with us." When Joseph woke up, he did what the angel of the Lord had commanded him and took Mary home as his wife. But he had no union with her until she gave birth to a son. And he gave him the name Jesus.*

1. How did Joseph initially react to the news that Mary was pregnant?

    _____

    _____

    _____

    _____

2. Mary was not the only one who exhibited faith in God's plan. Based on this passage, what character qualities do you think Joseph possessed?

    _____

    _____

    _____

    _____

3. Joseph knew that others would assume he had gotten Mary pregnant. Unless he divorced her, his reputation would be at stake for the rest of his life. So Joseph's obedience to God cost him the right to hold on to his own reputation. How does this show the depth of Joseph's faith in God?

    _____

    _____

    _____

    _____

4. What action did Joseph take as a result of his faith?

    _____

    _____

    _____

    _____

dig

Mary demonstrated her faith in three main ways: (1) Her heart and mind were open and available to hearing from God, (2) she believed God when she heard from Him, and (3) she acted on what God had revealed to her. Let's examine each of these three areas in which she demonstrated faith.

available

The first way that Mary exhibited her faith in God was by telling Him that she was available to be used by Him for whatever purposes He had planned.

1. Although the Bible doesn't tell us for sure, most scholars believe that Mary was a teenager when the angel spoke to her. If you were Mary and you had just received this message from the angel, how would you have reacted to the news?

2. Faith means being open to what God wants to do in our lives. How was Mary open and available to be used by God?

3. What are ways in which God has used people your age?

believing

Notice that not only did Mary open her heart and mind to hearing from the Lord, but she also believed what the angel was telling her. Although she might have questioned how she could give birth to the Messiah, she never doubted that the angel's words to her were true. She exhibited faith that what he said would come to pass.

1. What obstacles could have stood in the way of Mary believing the message from the angel? What did she do when she had doubts?

   _____

   _____

   _____

2. How do the following verses relate to the type of faith that Mary showed?

   Romans 4:20-21

   _____

   _____

   _____

   Hebrews 11:1

   _____

   _____

   _____

committed to action

Mary not only was open to hearing from God and believed what He said was true, but she also took the final step and acted on what the Lord had said to her.

1. What did Mary do immediately after the angel had left?

   _____

   _____

   _____

   _____

2. What did Elizabeth say about Mary's belief in what the angel had said to her? How did God use people in Mary's life to reinforce Mary's act of faith?

   _____

   _____

   _____

   _____

3. How did Mary's song of praise show that she was a willing participant in the plans that God had for her life and that she would act according to His will?

   _____

   _____

   _____

   _____

apply

So, what is faith all about, anyway? Consider the following true story of a young girl named Karen:

Sixteen-year-old Karen was lying in a coma in the community hospital. She had been in a horrible accident and was still on the critical list, but the doctors had not given up hope.

The same week that Karen was in the accident, her church was having an evangelistic crusade. The guest speaker was an evangelist and faith healer. The pastor of the church and Karen's parents asked the faith healer to come to the hospital to pray that Karen's health might be restored. He agreed to try.

They all went to Karen's hospital room, where she was literally being kept alive by a machine. The faith healer prayed, and in an excited voice claimed that God had healed Karen.

Karen's parents were ecstatic, and the pastor cried tears of joy. Yet Karen remained in a coma. The faith healer insisted that she had been healed and that as a demonstration of faith, her parents should ask the doctors to disconnect the life-support machine.

The doctors and nurses disagreed. Karen's parents went to court to get an order to force the hospital to disconnect the machine. Eventually, Karen was taken off the machine at the insistence of the family and a court of law.

Karen died three days later.[1]

1. What is your impression of this story?

_____

_____

_____

2. If you were Karen's parents or her pastor, how would you feel when Karen died?

_____

_____

_____

3. On what did each of the following people in the story base their faith?

    Karen's parents

    _____

    _____

    _____

    Karen's pastor

    _____

    _____

    _____

    The faith healer

    _____

    _____

    _____

4. What would you say to the faith healer? What if the faith healer told you that you just didn't have enough faith?

    _____

    _____

    _____

    _____

5. What does this story tell us about faith and about trusting in God?

    _____

    _____

    _____

    _____

6. Consider each of the following statements. Next to each
   statement, write T for true or F for false.

   ____   It is impossible to have faith in something you can't see.
   ____   Seeing is believing.
   ____   You only believe as much as you live.
   ____   Faith is a blind trust in something you hope for.
   ____   Faith is more fact than feeling.
   ____   Faith without obedience is not really faith at all.
   ____   Unanswered prayer is a sign of a lack of faith.
   ____   Doubt is just a lack of faith.
   ____   Everybody has faith in something.

7. Now read the following passages. According to these verses,
   on what is faith based? What would each of these descriptions of faith look like in the life of a young person today?

   Luke 1:45

   _____

   _____

   _____

   Romans 4:20-21

   _____

   _____

   _____

   Philippians 4:13

   _____

   _____

   _____

2 Timothy 1:12

_____

_____

_____

Hebrews 11:1

_____

_____

_____

James 2:17

_____

_____

_____

8. When was a time you demonstrated faith in God?

_____

_____

_____

9. When was a time you demonstrated a lack of faith in God?
   What can you do when you have doubts?

_____

_____

_____

_____

10. How can difficult situations build your faith in God?

_____

_____

_____

reflect

1. Matthew Henry defined faith as "a firm persuasion and expectation that God will perform all He has promised to us in Christ." In your own words, describe what having faith in Christ means in your life.

    _____

    _____

    _____

2. What are some things, other than God, in which you often place your faith? When is it difficult for you to trust God?

    _____

    _____

    _____

3. What are some of the roadblocks that keep you from having greater faith in God? How can you respond when you encounter one of those roadblocks?

    _____

    _____

    _____

4. In Matthew 17:20-21, Jesus said, "I tell you the truth, if you had faith as small as a mustard seed, you can say to this mountain, 'Move from here to there' and it will move. Nothing will be impossible for you." What is a "mountain" that needs to be moved in your life?

    _____

    _____

    _____

5. How will you make yourself available to God in this particular situation?

6. What do you need to trust God for in this situation? How can God's Word help you?

7. Who can you turn to for support as you walk in faith? How can you help each other trust God?

meditation

I have been crucified with Christ and I no longer live, but
Christ lives in me. The life I live in the body, I live by faith in
the Son of God, who loved me and gave himself for me.

GALATIANS 2:20

Note

1. Adapted from Jim Burns, *Youth Worker's Book of Case Studies* (Ventura, CA: Gospel Light), p. 50.

unit II

the heart of the new testament

The day was October 17. As my wife and I quietly slipped out of our room, we were praying that we wouldn't make a noise. We crept across the hallway and into the next room. There he was, having one of the most significant days of his little life, and didn't even know it. It was our son Joshua's first birthday. As we sang "Happy Birthday" to him, he looked at us as if we had lost our minds. It was his day, and we were going to go to his favorite place on earth—Disneyland! It was time for Joshua to experience his first ride at Disneyland. Joshua was a veteran of the park and had been almost everywhere inside, but he hadn't been on a ride until today.

My wife and I entered the park with Joshua and headed straight for the castle. Joshua's first ride would be the Dumbo ride. We climbed into the airborne elephant, and I strapped us in. In moments, we were in the air going up, and then going down! I had a great time. Unfortunately for Joshua, it was another story. As his few strands of hair blew in the wind, his face became a picture of sheer panic!

That night, after we laid Joshua in bed, still clutching his Mickey Mouse balloon, my wife and I prayed for Joshua. We prayed that God would look over his little life and guide him. We prayed that God would reveal His love to him and that he would come to know Christ. We prayed that Joshua would know that Mom and Dad loved him with all their hearts.

After we quietly crept out of his room, I went downstairs and sat in our living room. I pulled out my journal and began to write. I wrote Joshua a letter, telling him how much I loved him. I told him what he meant to me and how my life would never be the same since God gave him to us as a gift. I told him of my prayers for him and what type of dad I wanted to be for him. I wrote and I cried. I wrote and I poured my heart out to my son whom I loved with all my heart.

In its purest form, that is what the Bible is: God's love letter letting us know how much He loves us. It's a glimpse into our Father's heart. The kids we work with need to see it, be exposed to it and be changed and moved by it. The students that we work with need to listen to their heavenly Father's heart as He pours out His love for them within the pages of His Word.

I believe that one of the callings of the youth worker is to bring kids into contact with the living Word of God. It's a message from the Father's heart to ours. So as you lead your students through the heart of the New Testament, listen carefully. The heartbeat you hear is your heavenly Father's.

the incredible, unconditional love of God

For God so loved the world, that he gave . . .
JOHN 3:16

"I love you." Three simple words define the unfathomable nature of God. What can you, as an adult who has a love for God and a love for teenagers, do to put the two together? You can teach, live, exemplify, recite, promise, model, proclaim, reach, pray, find and display the unconditional love of God. What does it mean when God says, "I love you"? Simply and profoundly stated, it means, "I love you, period."

I states the personal nature of God's love for us. The personal pronoun I identifies God. When you use the word "I," you must be present, delivering the message one on one to the other individual. For instance, if we were to tell another person, "I've heard it said that 'I love you' is a message God wants to give to you," the communiqué would be valuable, but it would put emphasis on our integrity, intelligence and insight. As much as we might like to overrate these three qualities in our lives, I am sure the other person would rather hear the message straight from the One who spoke it in the first place. God wants to tell us, "*I* love you."

Love is the verb—the action. God's incredible, unconditional love is not just an emotion or a descriptive term, but also an action. Young people need to see to believe, and God's personal love will be made real to them through powerful action.

You is the object of the statement. The active love of a personal God is given directly to you and to me. Young people are desperately searching for love. They pay to watch other people love each other in movies. They plug in to hear people sing about love in songs. Deep inside, they wonder if they will ever experience exclusive love from someone else. That's why marriage continues to be a trendy institution. What kid doesn't want to be the object of the I-love-you message?

"I love you." Notice that the statement is punctuated with a period. The death of Christ is the period at the end of God's "I love you." Paul says, "But God demonstrates his own love for us in this: While we were still sinners, Christ died for us" (Romans 5:8). The love of God is finalized in the cross of Jesus Christ. There are no *ifs*, *ands* or *buts* to this message of love.

May God's message of His incredible, unconditional, personal, active love be the hallmark of your ministry. Kids are dying to hear it, and God died to share it.

It is another's fault if he be ungrateful; but it is mine if I do not give.
SENECA

the incredible, unconditional love of God

starter

WHAT'S LOVE GOT TO DO WITH IT? Before your meeting, prepare four grocery-size paper bags with the following titles written in permanent markers on the outside of each:

Bag One:	Beauty
Bag Two:	Brains
Bag Three:	Bucks
Bag Four:	Brawn

Fill each bag with objects that would represent those areas of our lives (be creative). Below are some examples:

Beauty	mirror, make-up, clothes, weights, comb, magazine covers
Brains	diploma, calculator, business card, *Wall Street Journal*
Bucks	money, toy car, credit cards, jewelry, vacation guides, pictures of possessions
Brawn	sports equipment, trophies, awards, pictures of athletes

Divide your group into four fairly equal groups and give each group one of the bags. Explain that each bag represents an area that people use to gain value, acceptance and love in their lives. Explain that inside each bag are items that physically represent those areas. Have each group go through the bag and then answer the following questions. When groups have finished, have them come back together and share a few of their items and their answers.

1. How does each item in your bag represent this area of life?

   ----

2. How does the world attach value to this area of life?

   ----

3.   How is God's love different from the world's version of love?

_____

_____

_____

_____

message

God has an incredible, unconditional, never-ending love for each of us. No matter who we are, no matter where we've been, no matter what has happened to us and no matter what we've done, God is ready with His arms open wide to welcome us home. Understanding and accepting God's love can be one of the toughest things to do. Nevertheless, one fact remains: God loves us! Throughout the New Testament, God gives us "snapshots" that reveal His love to us. Today, we will take a look at three such snapshots: (1) the incredible love of God, (2) the unconditional love of God, and (3) the personal nature of the love of God.

the incredible love of God

The first snapshot we see demonstrates the incredible nature of God's love for us. Read the following story of the woman who was brought to Jesus in John 8:1-11:

But Jesus went to the Mount of Olives. At dawn he appeared again in the temple courts, where all the people gathered around him, and he sat down to teach them. The teachers of the law and the Pharisees brought in a woman caught in adultery. They made her stand before the group and said to Jesus, "Teacher, this woman was caught in the act of adultery. In the Law Moses commanded us to stone such women. Now what do you say?" They were using this question as a trap, in order to have a basis for accusing him.

But Jesus bent down and started to write on the ground with his finger. When they kept on questioning him, he straightened up and said to them, "If any one of you is without sin, let him be the first to throw a stone at her." Again he stooped down and wrote on the ground.

At this, those who heard began to go away one at a time, the older ones first, until only Jesus was left, with the woman still standing there. Jesus straightened up and asked her, "Woman, where are they? Has no one condemned you?"

"No one, sir," she said. "Then neither do I condemn you," Jesus declared. "Go now and leave your life of sin."

1. Why was the woman brought to Jesus?

   _____

   _____

   _____

2. How did Jesus respond to the teachers of the law and the Pharisees, who had brought her?

   _____

   _____

   _____

   _____

3. How does Jesus' final statements to her reflect God's incredible love?

   _____

   _____

   _____

   _____

the unconditional love of God

Not only is God's love incredible, but it is also unconditional. We see a snapshot of this in the Parable of the Lost Son that Jesus told in Luke 15:11-24:

There was a man who had two sons. The younger one said to his father, "Father, give me my share of the estate." So he divided his property between them.

Not long after that, the younger son got together all he had, set off for a distant country and there squandered his wealth in wild living. After he had spent everything, there was a severe famine in that whole country, and he began to be in need. So he went and hired himself out to a citizen of that country, who sent him to his fields to feed pigs. He longed to fill his stomach with the pods that the pigs were eating, but no one gave him anything.

When he came to his senses, he said, "How many of my father's hired men have food to spare, and here I am starving to death! I will set out and go back to my father and say to him: Father, I have sinned against heaven and against you. I am no longer worthy to be called your son; make me like one of your hired men." So he got up and went to his father.

But while he was still a long way off, his father saw him and was filled with compassion for him; he ran to his son, threw his arms around him and kissed him.

The son said to him, "Father, I have sinned against heaven and against you. I am no longer worthy to be called your son."

But the father said to his servants, "Quick! Bring the best robe and put it on him. Put a ring on his finger and sandals on his feet. Bring the fattened calf and kill it. Let's have a feast and celebrate. For this son of mine was dead and is alive again; he was lost and is found." So they began to celebrate.

1. What was the younger son's attitude at the beginning of
    the story? What happened to change his attitude?

    _____

    _____

    _____

    _____

2. How did the father respond to his son coming home?

    _____

    _____

    _____

    _____

3. How did the son feel about the reception he received?

    _____

    _____

    _____

    _____

4. How does this story reflect the unconditional love of God?

    _____

    _____

    _____

    _____

the personal nature of the love of God

Finally, we see the personal nature of God's love in snapshots of
Scripture such as John 3:16-17 and Romans 5:5-8:

> *For God so loved the world that he gave his one and only Son, that
> whoever believes in him shall not perish but have eternal life. For*

God did not send his Son into the world to condemn the world, but to save the world through him (John 3:16-17).

And hope does not disappoint us, because God has poured out his love into our hearts by the Holy Spirit, whom he has given us. You see, at just the right time, when we were still powerless, Christ died for the ungodly. Very rarely will anyone die for a righteous man, though for a good man someone might possibly dare to die. But God demonstrates his own love for us in this: While we were still sinners, Christ died for us (Romans 5:5-8).

1. According to John 3:16-17, why did God send His Son into the world?

_____

_____

_____

_____

3. According to Romans 5:5-8, how has God poured His love into us?

_____

_____

_____

_____

4. How did God personally demonstrate His love for us?

_____

_____

_____

_____

dig

1. Has there ever been a time when you felt that God didn't love you because of something that happened to you, or that He couldn't possibly love you because of something you've done wrong? Explain.

   _____

   _____

   _____

   _____

2. What is the difference between a love that is based on who you are and not what you do?

   _____

   _____

   _____

   _____

3. What makes it so difficult to understand or accept the love of God?

   _____

   _____

   _____

   _____

4. How can any person experience God's love personally (see John 3:16)?

   _____

   _____

   _____

   _____

apply

Each of us, at one time or another, has questioned why God would allow certain events to happen in our lives. Doesn't He care about how we feel? Doesn't He love us anymore? Why isn't He helping us? Imagine for a moment that you had a best friend named Brian who was dealing with some personal issues in his life that was causing him to ask these types of questions. Read the following scenario, and then consider how you would address your friend's questions about the love of God.

The bell rings just as you slip into your chair. As you pull your homework out of your book, you lean over to talk to Brian, one of your friends since fifth grade. He tells you that he needs to talk to you after class and that it's really important. As you lean back into your chair, you notice the expression on Brian's face. He looks angry and frustrated, but also a bit lost.

You and Brian have done everything together: vacations, church events, everything. Brian gets along with his parents. He has told you, "They're okay. We get into fights every once in a while, but for the most part we get along." But lately you've seen some changes. Brian's parents have been fighting more and more. In fact, a few weeks ago Brian said they were yelling, fighting and throwing stuff.

The bell rings and you head out of class with Brian close behind. As the two of you round the building going out toward the field, Brian opens up and says, "My parents are getting a divorce!"

"What! You've got to be kidding!" you exclaim.

"They told me before school today."

As you lean against the building, Brian starts to cry and says, "It's all I've thought about all day long. How could this have happened? I thought my parents loved each other, and now they're getting a divorce! Don't they even care about how I feel? Doesn't anyone care about how I feel? How could God let this happen? Doesn't He love us anymore? I pray for my parents, but why isn't God helping? Can't my parents see how much I hurt? Can't God see? Where is He when I need Him? Where is this God who supposedly loves me?"

1. What would you say to Brian?

   _____

   _____

   _____

2. How would you explain God's love to Brian?

   _____

   _____

   _____

3. In Romans 8:38-39, Paul writes, "For I am convinced that neither death nor life, neither angels nor demons, neither the present nor the future, nor any powers, neither height nor depth, nor anything else in all creation, will be able to separate us from the love of God that is in Christ Jesus our Lord." What does this say about God's love?

   _____

   _____

   _____

   _____

4. How does this passage apply to Brian's situation?

    ....

    ....

    ....

    ....

    ....

5. What kinds of circumstances keep you from experiencing
    God's love? What does God promise in Romans 8:39?

    ....

    ....

    ....

    ....

    ....

6. How can this picture of God's love affect the way you feel
    about yourself?

    ....

    ....

    ....

    ....

    ....

7. God's radical love for us calls for a response. How can you
    respond to God's love today?

    ....

    ....

    ....

    ....

    ....

reflect

1. In what area of your life do you need to experience more of the incredible, unconditional, personal love of God?

   _____

   _____

   _____

   _____

2. Below are some passages about the love that God has for you. Read the passages and then complete the statements.

Psalm 86:5	God's love is:	_____
John 3:16-17	God's love is:	_____
Romans 5:5-8	God's love is:	_____
Romans 8:38-39	God's love is:	_____
Ephesians 2:4-6	God's love is:	_____
1 John 3:1	God's love is:	_____
1 John 4:8-10	God's love is:	_____

3. How can knowing the depth of God's love for you impact the way you see yourself and others?

   _____

   _____

   _____

   _____

   _____

4. How can you be a light for the love of God . . .

In your family?

_____
_____
_____
_____

At school and work?

_____
_____
_____
_____

In your community?

_____
_____
_____
_____

In your church?

_____
_____
_____
_____

In your sport, club or extracurricular activity?

_____
_____
_____
_____

5. Spend a couple of minutes writing a letter to God, telling Him how you feel about His love, your relationship with Him, and your gratitude and thankfulness to Him.

Dear God,

_____

_____

_____

_____

_____

_____

_____

_____

Love Always,

_____

meditation

And I pray that you, being rooted and established in love, may have power, together with all the saints, to grasp how wide and long and high and deep is the love of Christ, and to know this love that surpasses knowledge—that you may be filled to the measure of all the fullness of God.

EPHESIANS 3:17-19

the amazing grace of God

But the gift is not like the trespass. For if the many died by the trespass of the one man, how much more did God's grace and the gift that came by the grace of the one man, Jesus Christ, overflow to the many!

ROMANS 5:15

Mr. Kim, an eighth-grade math teacher, began many of his classes with classical music. Not a single 14-year-old in his class was about to admit a liking for Mr. Kim's choice of entertainment. When you're in junior high, culture goes as deep as the acceptance level of your peers.

Todd, one of the students, had a successful year in Mr. Kim's class. Math came easier for him than most of the other students, so he rose to the top of the class, but not without hard work. No one got off easy in Mr. Kim's class. At the end of the year, Todd was in line for the eighth-grade math student-of-the-year award. He was delighted in spite of the ribbing from a few classmates.

Unfortunately, Todd's laziness clouded his judgment. He decided that he could miss out on a final class. He had already bagged an *A* and the award was his, so he reasoned that he didn't need to bother with the last class. However, as he was sitting out on the school lawn, a classmate found him and said that Mr. Kim was looking for him. "You're in trouble for ditching class," the classmate added.

Well, Todd wasn't quite ditching; he just wasn't showing up for work that he figured he had already finished. Mr. Kim didn't buy the excuse. "Do you want to take your hard work and your award and throw it away in one day?" he asked Todd.

Mr. Kim's track record was not laced with grace. He was a tough teacher. But in Todd's case, Mr. Kim extended forgiveness, and Todd received the math award after all. Yet Todd's fly-the-coop swan song discredited an attitude in keeping with the award. Even though he received an *A* in the class, students don't get awarded for skipping class. Mr. Kim's grace gave Todd something he didn't deserve—regardless of his "good" past.

Have you ever had a time when you received something you really didn't deserve? That's called grace. Grace is a gift that God extends to us, not an honor that He bestows on us for our supposed "good" work. Kids today need grace and forgiveness, even though they might deserve to be dropped from the ceremony. While there are no perfect students, God continues to bring us along with His love. He's the one standing in the audience and applauding when our name is called.

If you judge people, you have no time to love them.
MOTHER TERESA

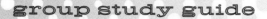

the amazing grace of God

starter

COIN GIVEAWAY: Provide enough quarters to the students in your group so that everyone can have four or five. Tell students that on the count of three, their job will be to give away as many of the quarters as they can. However, as they do so, they must follow these two rules: (1) they can only give one quarter away at a time, and (2) they must take any quarter given to them. Give the members about two or three minutes to give away as many coins as they can. After the allotted time is up, discuss the following questions:

1. How did you feel when you gave away money?

   ....

   ....

   ....

Note: You can download this group study guide in 8¹/₂" x 11" format at
www.gospellight.com/uncommon/the_new_testament.zip.

2. How did it feel to receive money?

    ....

    ....

    ....

3. What are some things that God has given you just because
    He loves you, even though you don't deserve it?

    ....

    ....

    ....

4. How would you explain the word "grace" to someone?

    ....

    ....

    ....

message

God's grace is amazing because He offers it freely to us and because without it, it would be impossible for us to have eternal life
with Christ. Our hearts are established by grace, we are justified
by grace, our service is rendered acceptable by grace, and we are
comforted by grace. What's more, God gives us grace not because
we deserve it but because He loves us. God is a God of grace, giving us that which we don't deserve. In Ephesians 2:1-10, Paul
talks about this gift that God gives to each of us:

> *As for you, you were dead in your transgressions and sins, in which
> you used to live when you followed the ways of this world and of the
> ruler of the kingdom of the air, the spirit who is now at work in*

those who are disobedient. All of us also lived among them at one time, gratifying the cravings of our sinful nature and following its desires and thoughts. Like the rest, we were by nature objects of wrath. But because of his great love for us, God, who is rich in mercy, made us alive with Christ even when we were dead in transgressions—it is by grace you have been saved. And God raised us up with Christ and seated us with him in the heavenly realms in Christ Jesus, in order that in the coming ages he might show the incomparable riches of his grace, expressed in his kindness to us in Christ Jesus. For it is by grace you have been saved, through faith—and this not from yourselves, it is the gift of God—not by works, so that no one can boast. For we are God's workmanship, created in Christ Jesus to do good works, which God prepared in advance for us to do.

From this passage, we see that grace is a gift of life, love, salvation and a future. Let's look at each of these aspects of grace in turn.

grace is a gift of life

1. According to this passage, what were we dead in? Who did we used to follow?

    ----

2. What did God do out of His great love for us?

    ----

grace is a gift of love

1. How does Paul describe our condition before God made
    us alive in Christ?

    _____

    _____

    _____

    _____

    _____

2. Why did God raise us up with Christ? How does this show
    His love?

    _____

    _____

    _____

    _____

grace is a gift of salvation

1. What does Paul mean when he says "it is by grace you have
    been saved"?

    _____

    _____

    _____

    _____

2. Why did God save you by grace through faith?

    _____

    _____

    _____

    _____

grace is a gift of a future

1. What do you think it means to be "God's workmanship"?

   ....

   ....

   ....

   ....

2. Note that at the end of this passage, Paul states that we are "created in Christ Jesus to do good works, which God prepared in advance for us to do." How does this reflect the grace of God?

   ....

   ....

   ....

   ....

dig

So, when we accept God's gift of grace into our lives, how does that affect us? What changes take place in terms of the way we act and lead our lives? In Romans 5:1-5 and 18-21, the apostle Paul describes several ways in which our lives are different as a result of God's grace:

> *Therefore, since we have been justified through faith, we have peace with God through our Lord Jesus Christ, through whom we have gained access by faith into this grace in which we now stand. And we rejoice in the hope of the glory of God. Not only so, but we also rejoice in our sufferings, because we know that suffering produces perseverance; perseverance, character; and character, hope. And hope does not disappoint us, because God has poured out his*

love into our hearts by the Holy Spirit, whom he has given us. . . .
Consequently, just as the result of one trespass was condemnation
for all men, so also the result of one act of righteousness was justi-
fication that brings life for all men. For just as through the dis-
obedience of the one man the many were made sinners, so also
through the obedience of the one man the many will be made righ-
teous. The law was added so that the trespass might increase. But
where sin increased, grace increased all the more, so that, just as
sin reigned in death, so also grace might reign through righteousness
to bring eternal life through Jesus Christ our Lord.

1. Based on these verses, what are some of the benefits that
   we can enjoy because of God's grace?

   ....
   ....
   ....

2. How do these verses describe the life a person can have
   with God?

   ....
   ....
   ....
   ....

3. How can living in God's grace give purpose to suffering?
   What result can suffering have in the life of someone who
   puts his or her hope in God?

   ....
   ....
   ....
   ....

4. To whom is God's grace available?

5. What effect can grace have on sin?

6. Why is it important that grace is a gift? How does the fact
    that God's grace is a gift influence the quality of the life
    God gives to a person?

7. What are some ways people try to attain salvation?

8. How does it feel to know that you are loved by your Cre-
    ator no matter who you are or what you've done?

apply

Read the following story about Father Maximilian Kolbe, a Polish priest who was imprisoned in Auschwitz, a German concentration camp, during World War II.

It was a cold, overcast day as I stood in front of Cell 21 in the basement of Barracks 11—the Death Block. What stood before me was a memorial to one of the most extraordinary people and events in all of Auschwitz—Father Maximilian Kolbe.

Father Maximilian Kolbe was a Catholic priest sentenced to be imprisoned in Auschwitz in May 1941. Upon his arrival at KL Auschwitz, he was informed that the life expectancy of a priest was about a month in Auschwitz. Father Kolbe took it upon himself to be an agent of love within the dismal hopelessness of the barbed wire fences.

One night in July 1941, amidst the sounds of motorcycles and barking dogs, a man from Barracks 14 escaped from Auschwitz. The next morning as the prisoners lined up for morning roll call, they noticed the gallows in front of them—empty. The escapee had succeeded, yet someone would pay the price for him. That morning, 10 men were selected to die in the starvation bunker inside the Death Block. One of those men was 5659. As the ten were being led away to screams of horror, a small, frail man stepped forward. His number was 16670. His name was Father Maximilian Kolbe.

"Sir, I'd like to die in place of one of those men."

"In whose place do you want to die?" asked the Commander.

"For that one." Father Kolbe lifted his finger and pointed at 5659. And in an instant, 5659 was erased off the death ledger and 16670 was entered. One life for another—a gift of life. On August 14, 1941, in a starvation bunker known only as Cell 21 in the basement of Barracks 11, one man gave the gift of life by dying in place of another. Number 16670 died in place of 5659.

As I peered through the bars into the starvation cell where Maximilian Kolbe died, I felt as if I were on holy ground. The plaque on the wall of the cell and the memorial fire in the center of the cell pointed to what was one of the most extraordinary events in the history of this place called Auschwitz. Here was light in the darkness, love afloat in the middle of a sea of hate, and hope in the midst of madness. As I stood at the place where one man gave his life for another in an act of love—the gift of life— I was broken and changed.

It was a cold, overcast day when another Man gave His life. He was Light in the darkness, Love afloat in the middle of a sea of hate, and Hope in the midst of madness. On that hill, Jesus gave His life for all humanity—not only for all humankind but also more specifically for you and me. A gift of life and an act of love given because of God's incredible love for you and me.

Too often I lose sight of God's love and His grace. Too often I get so wrapped up in my busyness for Him that I miss the opportunity to be with Him. Standing in front of that cell, I was brought face to face with the radical love that God has for you and for me. God loved you and me so much that He couldn't stand to live without us for eternity. It was a love that drove Him to action—a love that drove Jesus Christ to die on a cross for you and me. That's the message of the New Testament.

As I walked away from that moment in time at the starvation cell where Father Maximilian Kolbe gave his life for another, I wondered about 5659. Who was he? What went through his mind as he saw Father Kolbe being led away to his death, while he was given the gift of life? I walked away from the basement of Barracks 11 broken—and changed. Broken, that a man would give his life for another—changed in my gratitude for what was done for me on Calvary. Just like 5659, I was being led away to my death when another Man stepped forward out of the crowd. Looking into my eyes, He saw the terror and the pain.

"Sir, I'd like to die in the place of one of those men," He said.

"In whose place do you want to die?"

"For that one."

Just as Father Maximilian Kolbe, 16670, gave the gift of life to prisoner 5659, so Jesus Christ has given us the gift of life and of grace. For just as prisoner 5659 experienced a radical grace—a gift that was never deserved—so do we experience a gift that we do not deserve: the amazing grace of God!

1. How does the story of Father Maximilian Kolbe illustrate the grace of God? What do you think motivated him to give the gift of life to someone?

    ----

2. What are some things God has given or done for you or
    your family "just because," even though you didn't de-
    serve it? How did you respond?

    _____

    _____

    _____

    _____

3. Think about someone who needs to experience God's
    grace (you can include yourself). What effect could God's
    gift of grace have on that life?

    _____

    _____

    _____

    _____

reflect

1. What is one thing that has challenged or surprised you
    from this session on God's grace?

    _____

    _____

    _____

    _____

2. What is one area in which you need to experience more of
    God's grace?

    _____

    _____

    _____

    _____

3. Someone once said that "mercy is not getting what you do deserve. Grace is getting what you don't deserve." What does receiving God's grace mean to you?

----

4. Why is it often so difficult for us to understand and accept God's grace? Why do you need God's grace? What can God's grace in your life look like?

----

5. Who in your life needs to hear and see the message of God's grace? What would you tell him or her? How can you show God's grace to that person?

----

meditation

And as God's grace reaches more and more
people, there will be great thanksgiving, and God will
receive more and more glory.

2 CORINTHIANS 4:15

being a part of
God's family

In Christ we who are many form one body, and each member
belongs to all the others.

ROMANS 12:5

Whenever the National Football League holds its annual drafts, the first round, top-five draft choices always draw big attention. These highly acclaimed and soon-to-be-well-paid college students are in a position to be the league's newest celebrities. The cover of sports pages across the nation will soon be pictorial and verbal trophies to these top kids. Virtually every time the new player and soon-to-be-star is picked, he or she is quickly issued a team jersey, team hat and number.

What would it be like if we, the Church, gave the same attention to welcoming new believers into the family of God? What if a new Christian received a party at the next church service? We would call his or her name, take pictures and speak clearly into the microphone for all to hear what a wonderful joy it is to have him or her on God's team. Churches would experience the incredible joy God feels every time someone new is added to His family.

Perhaps another sports tradition that could be worked into the fabric of churches even more readily than the draft celebration is the moment after a player is called for a foul or penalty. The referee states something like, "Number 62, illegal use of hands on offense—10-yard penalty." Now there is a picture for the church. "Mr. John Doe, husband of Jane, illegal use of company funds—immediate dismissal from the job—continual sneers from church members behind his back—10-year penalty and recovery period."

In sports, the whole team suffers when one player incurs a penalty. According to Paul's words in Romans, the same is true in the Body of Christ: We each belong to each other, sharing in each other's pain and rejoicing in each other's successes. All too often in today's churches, when members go anywhere—either up or down—they tend to go there alone. It often seems easier to focus on a believer's sin than to celebrate a new believer's salvation or success.

If we overlook God's Word, we miss the power of being a part of God's people. Christianity is not just a right relationship with God or a guarantee of going to heaven. According to Scripture, becoming a believer means stepping into God's family. When the disciples asked Jesus to teach them how to talk to God, He told them to begin their prayer with "Our Father," and He remained in the third person, using words like "us," "we" and "our." God has always and will always look at us as a family in faith with one Father.

One truly affectionate soul in a family will exert a sweetening and harmonizing influence upon all its members.

HENRY VAN DYKE

being a part of
God's family

starter

THE PUZZLE OF THE FAMILY OF GOD: Buy or borrow a small child's puzzle (with approximately 12 pieces). Hand out the puzzle pieces to volunteers, one piece per volunteer. Ask each student to describe in detail from that one piece what the picture of the puzzle is. Then have the group of volunteers come together and build the puzzle. Discuss the questions that follow.

1. What can you tell about the puzzle from just one piece?

   _____

   _____

   _____

2. Why is every piece of the puzzle important? What if some pieces are missing?

_____

_____

_____

_____

3. What are some similarities between the puzzle and being a part of the family of God?

_____

_____

_____

_____

4. Is being a part of a church necessary to a Christian? Why or why not?

_____

_____

_____

_____

5. What are the advantages of being plugged into the family of God?

_____

_____

_____

_____

As an option, you could now give each person in the group a piece of another puzzle to symbolize that he or she belongs to the group and to God's puzzle: the Body of Christ.

message

When we become Christians, we become a part of the Body of Christ—the family of God. As a part of God's family, we have a responsibility to accept, love and care for one another. The Body of Christ is like a family, and family members need to feel that they belong, that they have unique parts or responsibilities, and that others care about them. Paul spoke about this in the following passage in 1 Corinthians 12:12-27:

> *The body is a unit, though it is made up of many parts; and though all its parts are many, they form one body. So it is with Christ. For we were all baptized by one Spirit into one body—whether Jews or Greeks, slave or free—and we were all given the one Spirit to drink.*
>
> *Now the body is not made up of one part but of many. If the foot should say, "Because I am not a hand, I do not belong to the body," it would not for that reason cease to be part of the body. And if the ear should say, "Because I am not an eye, I do not belong to the body," it would not for that reason cease to be part of the body. If the whole body were an eye, where would the sense of hearing be? If the whole body were an ear, where would the sense of smell be? But in fact God has arranged the parts in the body, every one of them, just as he wanted them to be. If they were all one part, where would the body be? As it is, there are many parts, but one body.*
>
> *The eye cannot say to the hand, "I don't need you!" And the head cannot say to the feet, "I don't need you!" On the contrary, those parts of the body that seem to be weaker are indispensable, and the parts that we think are less honorable we treat with special honor. And the parts that are unpresentable are treated with special modesty, while our presentable parts need no special treatment. But God has combined the members of the body and has given greater honor to the parts that lacked it, so that there should*

be no division in the body, but that its parts should have equal concern for each other. If one part suffers, every part suffers with it; if one part is honored, every part rejoices with it.

Now you are the body of Christ, and each one of you is a part of it.

Note in this passage that Paul states that within the Body of Christ, everyone belongs, everyone is needed, and everyone should be cared for. We will look at each of these points in turn.

everybody belongs

1. Why are the parts of the Body dependent on each other?

    _____

    _____

    _____

    _____

2. What happens when a part of the Body is missing or tries to live independent of the whole? What would this kind of Body look like?

    _____

    _____

    _____

    _____

3. What makes us part of the same Body? Who can be included as a part of the Body?

    _____

    _____

    _____

    _____

everybody is needed

1. Why is every part needed in the Body?

2. Is any part of the Body more important than any other part? How are they made equal?

3. Who decides how the Body is put together?

everybody is cared for

1. According to Paul, what should our attitude be toward others in the family of God?

2. What effect does it have on the Body if one part suffers?

    _____

    _____

    _____

    _____

3. What effect does it have on the whole Body if one part does well?

    _____

    _____

    _____

    _____

dig

The Body of Christ is the Church, with a capital C, and is made up of all followers of Christ, regardless of what church building they happen to gather in. Does Paul's concept of the Body of Christ match what you've seen in your particular church or youth group? Why or why not? Consider the following questions in light of what you've experienced.

1. What are some things that you've seen that keep people from feeling as if they belong to a group?

    _____

    _____

    _____

    _____

2. Paul states that "God has arranged the parts in the body, every one of them, just as he wanted them to be" (v. 18).

What does that mean for your group and also for you personally?

_____

_____

_____

_____

3. Why do you think that God gives different roles to people in the family of God?

_____

_____

_____

_____

4. Why is every part needed in the Body of Christ?

_____

_____

_____

_____

_____

5. Part of being needed in the Body of Christ means being responsible for others in the church. According to the following passages, what are some of the ways that we are to be responsible for our fellow believers in Christ?

Romans 12:4-5,10

_____

_____

_____

_____

Galatians 6:2

_____

_____

_____

_____

Ephesians 4:16

_____

_____

_____

_____

Philippians 2:1-5

_____

_____

_____

_____

Hebrews 10:24-25

_____

_____

_____

_____

6. What can happen when members of the Body of Christ don't do their parts? What impact can the Body of Christ have when everyone works together?

_____

_____

_____

7. Why do Christians often think of some people as being more important in the Body of Christ than others? What should your attitude be toward others in the family of God?

_____

_____

_____

_____

8. What does our love for each other say to those who don't belong to Christ?

_____

_____

_____

_____

apply

1. What can you do personally to help people feel like they belong?

_____

_____

_____

_____

2. What are some roles you can fill in your group to make it function more like a family?

_____

_____

_____

_____

3. What can your group do to make sure that everyone feels needed and is treated with equal value?

4. How can your group recognize the strengths of individual members? How can your group provide opportunities for everyone to serve?

5. What can your group do to care for the needs of others?

6. How can you be intentional about welcoming someone to our group on their first visit? How can you reach out to those in your group who are often overlooked?

7. What can you do when someone in the Body of Christ is difficult to care for?

_____

_____

_____

_____

reflect

1. What are some words that describe how you feel when you belong? When you feel needed? When you feel cared for?

_____

_____

_____

_____

2. On a scale of 1 to 10, rate how you feel that you are doing in each of these three areas.

Everybody belongs (everyone is of equal value).

1	2	3	4	5	6	7	8	9	10

I'm Weak Here   I'm Strong Here

Everybody is needed (everyone has a unique part or a unique responsibility).

1	2	3	4	5	6	7	8	9	10

I'm Weak Here   I'm Strong Here

Everybody is cared for (everyone has their needs met).

1	2	3	4	5	6	7	8	9	10

I'm Weak Here   I'm Strong Here

3. In which area do you need to do the most work? List three
    action steps you can take to improve in that area.

    1. _____
    2. _____
    3. _____

4. What strengths can you use to build up another follower
    of Christ?

    _____
    _____
    _____
    _____
    _____

meditation

Consequently, you are no longer foreigners
and aliens, but fellow citizens with God's people
and members of God's household, built on the
foundation of the apostles and prophets, with Christ
Jesus himself as the chief cornerstone.

EPHESIANS 2:19-20

being an agent of change

The kingdom of heaven is like yeast that a woman took and mixed into a large amount of flour until it worked all through the dough.

MATTHEW 13:33

In one of Jesus' parables, He told of a man who planted a mustard seed in his field. Although the mustard seed was incredibly small, when it was planted, it ultimately grew into a large tree in which the birds could come and perch (see Matthew 13:31-32). In the same way, though we may have a mustard-seed-sized faith, it can make a tree-sized impact in God's plan. In God's economy, quantity or scale is insignificant. A seemingly insignificant human who combines just a little faith with a big batch of God can make an incredible difference in a hurting world.

A husband-and-wife team once went on a mission trip to Haiti. The husband thoroughly enjoyed it, but the wife thoroughly hated it. She especially didn't like the time when she took a rickety old rowboat across a large bay to a small fishing village called Labadie. The oarsmen were friendly, the view was beautiful, and the water was a vibrant turquoise. However, as far as the wife was concerned, the bay was too deep and the boats too old and frail. She also didn't like the flight back across the small island of Haiti that she then had to take on a tiny nine-passenger aircraft. The drafty nature of the mountain-covered island provided quite an eventful ride. In fact, most of the passengers were rather grateful to touch down safely at the Port-au-Prince airport.

Even though the wife didn't enjoy the trip, it was admirable that she was willing to go in spite of her strong reservations. She had no faith in old boats and small planes, but her little bit of faith in a big God made the event a success. Her life since that trip became one of steady growth and impact for the kingdom of God. In fact, this mild-mannered woman and her husband launched a ministry in Eastern Europe. Not only did she raise her kids there, but she also gave birth to one there.

The couple's impact on thousands of lives, including many Eastern European teenagers, is an inspiration and an ongoing reminder of God's way of doing things. He doesn't need believers with a tree-sized faith to do great things for Him. He can take a small kernel of faith and use it to make a kingdom impact.

Every morning lean thine arms awhile upon the
windowsill of Heaven and gaze upon the Lord. Then, with that
vision in thine heart, turn strong to meet the day.
ANONYMOUS

being an agent of change

starter

SO WHERE'S GOD IN ALL THIS? Read the following account to the whole group and discuss the questions at the end.

They knew that they were in for a tough weekend when they had to step over the body of a drunken man to get into the hotel. Here they were in a rundown hotel a block from skid row in Los Angeles. As they entered the hotel, a stale, smoky smell greeted them. The team was here for a weekend of ministry and changing lives. Little did they know that the lives that would be changed were their own.

That night they were to tour the city—to allow God to break their hearts and to pray for the needs of the city. As they climbed into the blue Dodge van for the drive, the host asked, "Tonight, as you're looking around, ask yourself, *Where is God in all this? If God is a God of love, then why does He allow the things to happen that you're going to see tonight? Where is He and why does He seem to be silent?*"

As they drove the streets of inner-city Los Angeles, each person was affected by the scenes he or she saw: homeless women and children, drug deals, prostitutes, and fire barrels lit to provide some kind of warmth. As the van turned a corner, a prostitute was making a score and getting into a Jeep Cherokee, off to some unknown destination. During all of this time, the questions kept ringing in their ears: *Where is God in all this? Why does He seem to be silent?*

As the van arrived back at the hotel, the group shuffled into a small room off the lobby, all the while pondering these questions. The room was uncomfortably quiet as they struggled with their emotions, trying to find some answers. One by one, the students offered their opinions and thoughts. Then the host spoke up and said, "Where was God tonight? Was He silent? I'll tell you where God was tonight: He was riding in a blue Dodge van. The question is not where is God in all this and whether He cares, but where are God's people and do they really care enough to get involved in touching the world with His love."

1. What did the host mean when he said that God "was riding in a blue Dodge van"?

_____

_____

_____

_____

2. If you had been in that van, how would you have answered the questions posed to the students?

   _____

   _____

   _____

   _____

   _____

3. What are some situations around you in which God
   seems to be silent?

   _____

   _____

   _____

   _____

   _____

message

Christ calls each of us to be an agent of change in this world. His
desire is that we reach out to those around us and make a Kingdom impact one life at a time. All too often, we think that God
is only looking for "talented" individuals to do the work of His
Kingdom, when in fact He is just looking for those who are willing and available. God is looking for people who want to serve
in the small things—in the "whatevers." Making a difference
takes ordinary people doing ordinary things through the power
of an extraordinary God. Jesus captured this idea in a parable
that He told in Matthew 25:31-36. As you read this parable,
think about how what Jesus is saying applies to serving those in
need around us.

When the Son of Man comes in his glory, and all the angels with him, he will sit on his throne in heavenly glory. All the nations will be gathered before Him, and He will separate the people one from another as a shepherd separates the sheep from the goats. He will put the sheep on his right and the goats on his left.

Then the King will say to those on his right, "Come, you who are blessed by my Father; take your inheritance, the kingdom prepared for you since the creation of the world. For I was hungry and you gave me something to eat, I was thirsty and you gave me something to drink, I was a stranger and you invited me in, I needed clothes and you clothed me, I was sick and you looked after me, I was in prison and you came to visit me."

Then the righteous will answer him, "Lord, when did we see you hungry and feed you, or thirsty and give you something to drink? When did we see you a stranger and invite you in, or needing clothes and clothe you? When did we see you sick or in prison and go to visit you?"

The King will reply, "I tell you the truth, whatever you did for one of the least of these brothers of mine, you did for me."

Then he will say to those on his left, "Depart from me, you who are cursed, into the eternal fire prepared for the devil and his angels. For I was hungry and you gave me nothing to eat, I was thirsty and you gave me nothing to drink, I was a stranger and you did not invite me in, I needed clothes and you did not clothe me, I was sick and in prison and you did not look after me."

They also will answer, "Lord, when did we see you hungry or thirsty or a stranger or needing clothes or sick or in prison, and did not help you?"

He will reply, "I tell you the truth, whatever you did not do for one of the least of these, you did not do for me." Then they will go away to eternal punishment, but the righteous to eternal life.

1. List all the similarities and differences that you can find in
    this passage between the sheep and the goats.

    Similarities   Differences

    _____   _____

    _____   _____

    _____   _____

    _____   _____

2. What are some of the ways that the sheep served those
    around them?

    _____

    _____

    _____

    _____

3. Why do you think the sheep were so surprised when the
    King described everything they had done for him?

    _____

    _____

    _____

    _____

4. When the sheep and goats answer the King, what is the
    difference between their attitudes?

    _____

    _____

    _____

    _____

5. Who were the sheep really serving?

_____

_____

_____

6. Why do you think the goats never saw the face of Jesus in the needy ones around them?

_____

_____

_____

7. What do these verses imply about how we should feel regarding our service to others?

_____

_____

_____

dig

Helping those in need is evidence of our love and commitment to Christ. Being a Christian means being a part of God's plan to touch the world with His love. The clear voice of God calls us to reach out to others. It's more than words—it takes action!

1. What do the following passages say about making a difference for the Kingdom?

Matthew 25:40

_____

_____

_____

2 Corinthians 5:18-20

_____

_____

_____

_____

1 John 3:16-18

_____

_____

_____

_____

2. What attitude is Jesus describing when He says, "Whatever you did for one of the least of these brothers of mine, you did for me"?

_____

_____

_____

_____

3. In what ways are you often like the sheep in the story?

_____

_____

_____

_____

4. In what ways are you often like the goats?

_____

_____

_____

_____

apply

Sometimes, it is easy to be a servant to others, especially if the person whom we are assisting is grateful for our help. At other times, serving others can be a frustrating experience, especially if the person is indifferent or doesn't really care for our help. Regardless, whenever we serve, we need to focus on three main things: (1) being sensitive to the needs of others, (2) seeing the face of Jesus in those we are helping, and (3) serving with what we have and who we are.

being sensitive to the needs of others

1. What keeps us from being sensitive to the needs of those around us?

   _____

   _____

   _____

   _____

   _____

2. What are some of the needs you see in your group?

   _____

   _____

   _____

   _____

   _____

3. What are some ways these needs could be met?

   _____

   _____

   _____

   _____

seeing the face of Jesus in those we are helping

1. What do you think the statement, "When you're serving those around you, you are really serving Jesus Christ," means for a Christian?

    _____

    _____

    _____

    _____

2. How can this attitude change the way you approach people with needs?

    _____

    _____

    _____

    _____

serving with what you have and who you are

1. What are some ways in which people need to be cared for?

    _____

    _____

    _____

    _____

2. What are some things that you can do to make a difference in . . .

    Your church?

    _____

    _____

    _____

    _____

Your home?

_____

_____

_____

_____

Your school?

_____

_____

_____

_____

Your community?

_____

_____

_____

_____

reflect

1. God gives each of us gifts and abilities, and He expects us to use those to help others on His behalf. He also gives those who love Him a heart to meet needs using these gifts and abilities. What are some adjectives that describe how you typically feel when you notice someone with each of the following needs?

Homeless

_____

_____

_____

A visitor to school or church

_____

_____

_____

Sick or disabled

_____

_____

_____

_____

A prisoner (outcast)

_____

_____

_____

2. Does your list of adjectives seem to reflect the attitude of Jesus? Why or why not?

_____

_____

_____

_____

_____

3. What specific things can you do to be more sensitive to those in need?

_____

_____

_____

_____

_____

4. What are some simple ways that you can serve God with who you are and the gifts He has given you?

5. Who in your life has the "face of Jesus"? What is God calling you to do in this person's life?

6. If you could be involved in making an impact for God in any way, what would you do? (As you answer this question, keep Paul's words in Philippians 4:13 in mind: "I can do everything through Him who gives me strength.")

7. If you haven't done this, what is keeping you from doing so?

8. What does the statement, "making a difference takes ordinary people doing ordinary things through the power of an extraordinary God," mean to you?

_____

_____

_____

_____

_____

9. The following are some ideas for how you can make a difference in your world. As you look through the list, note your top three areas of interest:

- Volunteer in an area of ministry within your church
- Support a child through Compassion International (call 1-800-336-7676 or see www.compassion.com)
- Volunteer to work at a rescue mission
- Volunteer at a convalescent home
- Volunteer to work with a local ministry to the homeless in your area
- Support a missionary financially and in prayer
- Assist in a Sunday School class or with Vacation Bible School
- Write a note of encouragement to your pastor
- Go and visit a shut-in from your church
- Volunteer to greet visitors to your church on Sunday mornings
- Invite a new youth group member to join you and your friends for an activity
- Go on a short-term mission trip
- Volunteer with the Special Olympics

What are your top three areas of interest?

_____

_____

_____

_____

What are some other ideas you could pursue?

_____

_____

_____

_____

Pray about each of these areas and ask God to open the doors for you to get involved in one or all of them. Then . . . take action!

meditation

As the body without the spirit is dead,
so faith without deeds is dead.

JAMES 2:26

unit III
the message of the new testament

In the left-hand drawer of my desk I had what I called my "encouragement file." Within this file was every note of encouragement I had ever received during my time of ministry at my church. There were letters from students, parents, our senior pastor, volunteers and just about anybody who took the time to sit down and write a note. Why did I keep all these notes? I needed them!

When you're in the trenches of youth ministry, you need all the encouragement you can get. Too often, it seems too little. People rarely stop you just to say thanks, but when they do, it's something to savor. For me, there were days when I needed to go into my office, lock the door, pull out the encouragement file and be reminded of why I did what I did and what I was called to do. With all of the challenges that bombarded me in the trenches, there were times I needed to be refreshed and refocused on the task I had been called to do.

That's what the New Testament is all about. It is not only a love letter from the Father to His children, but it's also a letter of encouragement, refreshment and refocus. It's a letter to remind us that Christianity is not about what we do but about daring to be intimate with the Savior. It's a letter to remind us that God is still alive and active in our world today, changing lives, hearts and circumstances. It's a letter about what's important in life: loving God with all our hearts and showing that same love to others. It's a letter sent to help us refocus our hearts and to remind us to be ready at any moment for the return of Christ.

When the storms of life seem to rage out of control, we can anchor our souls to God's Word. It's a guide to help us reset our compass. In the same way, as you guide your students through the sections of the New Testament, your goal will be to help them anchor their lives to the Author of those pages. That way, when the storms come into their lives, making it so easy for them to lose heart, they can open the pages of His letter and be refreshed and refocused.

How can a young man keep his way pure? By living according to your word. I seek you with all my heart; do not let me stray from your commands. I have hidden your word in my heart that I might not sin against you.

PSALM 119:9-11

the gospels: a relationship instead of a religion

In the beginning was the Word, and the Word was with God,
and the Word was God. He was with God in the beginning. The Word
became flesh and made his dwelling among us.
JOHN 1:1-2,14

When people head off to college, chances are that their first apartment will be a dive. The construction may be more like a makeshift shack. Some apartments may have no heat. Some college students, in fact, have been known to turn on the oven and leave the door open and then sit on the door to find a touch of warmth. One ingenious roommate in particular was known to take his electric blanket when he got out of bed in the morning and drag it with him around the house, plugging it in to various outlets as he worked his way around the apartment.

If you want to get to know someone well, move in with that person into a small space. Make sure that some of the areas in that space are too low for you to stand upright. Share limited amenities, don't have any heat, and then stay put there with that other person for months. When you live in such a situation, it forces relationships out of the superficial levels.

The Gospels did not simply record the religious sayings of Jesus. Rather, the Gospels unveiled the presence of God when He moved in with humanity. He entered the world in an unheated stable with a wooden feedbox for a bed and animals for roommates. There was no glamour to be found in the circumstances of His birth, life or death.

Jesus came in humble, human form to bring a broken world into right relationship with a loving God. He was in a relationship as the Word and God before time. Out of this unity of God came the impetus to put aside the divine attributes, take on the humble markings of humanity, and dwell right here with us.

The religious principles are present in the Gospels, but the transforming power lies in the relationship. In Jesus' final hours before His death, He stated, "The world must learn that I love the Father" (John 14:31). If Jesus meant to start a religion, He chose the wrong mode of living to make His impact. Instead, He turned our attention to the love between His Father and Himself. He cared more about our hearts than His home. That's good news!

Many people begin coming to God once they stop being religious, because there is only one master of the heart—Jesus Christ, not religion.
OSWALD CHAMBERS

the gospels: a relationship instead of a religion

starter

LET ME ASK YOU A QUESTION: Divide students into groups of three or four and have them discuss each of the questions together. Then bring the groups back together to discuss their answers.

1. The time I felt closest to God was . . .

    _____

    _____

    _____

    _____

Note: You can download this group study guide in 8¹/₂" x 11" format at **www.gospellight.com/uncommon/the_new_testament.zip.**

2. When I became a Christian, I . . .

3. If I could see God face to face, I would ask Him . . .

4. I think having a relationship with God means . . .

5. When I think of being real with God, I think of . . .

message

The message of the Gospels is that God desires each and every person to have a vital, intimate relationship with Him, not just a stale religion. Christianity in its truest sense is daring to be intimate with God. Today, God is calling us to enter into a love relationship with Himself. In Matthew 5:1-10, Jesus gives us a glimpse in His Sermon on the Mount of exactly how we can be intimate with God:

> One day as he saw the crowds gathering, Jesus went up on the mountainside and sat down. His disciples gathered around him, and he began to teach them. "God blesses those who are poor and realize their need for him, for the Kingdom of Heaven is theirs. God blesses those who mourn, for they will be comforted. God blesses those who are humble, for they will inherit the whole earth. God blesses those who hunger and thirst for justice, for they will be satisfied. God blesses those who are merciful, for they will be shown mercy. God blesses those whose hearts are pure, for they will see God. God blesses those who work for peace, for they will be called the children of God. God blesses those who are persecuted for doing right, for the Kingdom of Heaven is theirs" (NLT).

From this passage, we see that being intimate with the Savior is marked by three things: (1) a radical brokenness, (2) a hunger for God, and (3) a heart for God and His work. We will examine each of these today more closely.

a radical brokenness

1. In this passage, Jesus says that God blesses those who are poor and realize their need for Him. What does God promise these individuals?

    _____

    _____

    _____

    _____

    _____

2. Why is it often difficult for us to admit that we are spiritually at the end of our rope and in need of a Savior?

_____

_____

_____

_____

_____

3. God wants us to be broken with the things that break His heart and for us to experience godly sorrow. How does this describe "those who mourn"?

_____

_____

_____

_____

_____

4. What are some of the things that break the heart of God?

_____

_____

_____

_____

_____

5. What does God promise to those who experience "godly sorrow"?

_____

_____

_____

_____

_____

6. Who are the "humble"? What does God promise to these individuals?

_____

_____

_____

_____

_____

a hunger for God

1. What does it mean to "hunger" and "thirst" for godly justice and righteousness?

_____

_____

_____

_____

_____

2. If we choose to hunger and thirst after God, what does He promise to do?

_____

_____

_____

_____

_____

a heart for God and his work

1. What is mercy?

_____

_____

_____

_____

2. How does God show mercy to people?

_____

_____

_____

_____

3. Why are the merciful blessed?

_____

_____

_____

_____

4. What are the characteristics of something that is pure?

_____

_____

_____

_____

5. Why can a person with a pure heart see God more clearly?

_____

_____

_____

_____

6. When a person works for peace, who's example is he or she following? Why is it work to bring peace?

_____

_____

_____

_____

7. What is the reward for those who are persecuted for doing right?

_____

_____

_____

_____

dig

Being a Christian means daring to be intimate with the Savior. Christianity is not about what church we may go to or what denomination we may belong to, but about having a living, vital and growing relationship with the one and only living God who knows us and desires for us to know Him.

For the word of God is living and active. Sharper than any double-edged sword, it penetrates even to dividing soul and spirit, joints and marrow; it judges the thoughts and attitudes of the heart (Hebrews 4:12).

1. According to this passage, what is the Word of God?

_____

_____

_____

_____

2. How does the Word of God help us to know God better?

_____

_____

_____

_____

But Jesus often withdrew to lonely places and prayed (Luke 5:16).

3. Why do you think Jesus liked to be alone when He prayed?

    _____

    _____

    _____

    _____

4. What are the benefits of praying alone in a quiet place?

    _____

    _____

    _____

    _____

Speak to one another with psalms, hymns and spiritual songs. Sing and make music in your heart to the Lord, always giving thanks to God the Father for everything, in the name of our Lord Jesus Christ (Ephesians 5:19-20).

5. How many ways to worship are described here?

    _____

    _____

    _____

    _____

    _____

6. How do attitude and worship influence each other?

    _____

    _____

    _____

    _____

Jesus called them together and said, "You know that the rulers of the Gentiles lord it over them, and their high officials exercise authority over them. Not so with you. Instead, whoever wants to become great among you must be your servant, and whoever wants to be first must be your slave—just as the Son of Man did not come to be served, but to serve, and to give his life as a ransom for many" (Matthew 20:25-28).

This is how we know what love is: Jesus Christ laid down his life for us. And we ought to lay down our lives for our brothers. If anyone has material possessions and sees his brother in need but has no pity on him, how can the love of God be in him? Dear children, let us not love with words or tongue but with actions and in truth (1 John 3:16-18).

7. What is our motivation for serving others?

_____

_____

_____

_____

8. How does serving others bring us closer to God?

_____

_____

_____

_____

apply

Sometimes, just a few feet can make all of the difference in the world. Consider the following story of Howard Carter and his crew, who in 1922 uncovered one of the greatest archaeological finds in history:

> In the Valley of the Kings stands a monument for all time—the tomb of King Tut. The excavation crew had spent years determining where the tomb was located. Finally, the day had come for them to start the dig. As the work progressed, the realization began to set in that they were in the wrong place. The tomb had to be located somewhere else in the valley.
>
> So, for the next 10 years, the excavation crew dug around the entire Valley of the Kings in search of the elusive tomb. One day, the leadership team sat down to refigure their calculations. After some discussion, they came to the conclusion that the tomb *must* be where they had begun digging almost 10 years before.
>
> As the crew reached the initial site where the quest began, the decision was made to dig around the site in hopes of possibly finding the entrance to the tomb. Days went by. Weeks went by.
>
> Finally, there was a breakthrough. One day, as they concentrated their efforts on one particular place, they unearthed the entrance to the tomb of King Tut. Incredible celebration set through the entire team—all except for the team leader. As he walked to a nearby tent, he began to cry. His assistant ran after him.
>
> "Why are you crying? We have just found perhaps the greatest treasure known to mankind!"
>
> "All these years we have been searching. Yet in the end, we have wasted 10 years of our lives for a matter of a few yards."

Sometimes, the longest distance to travel in the world is 12 inches—the distance from our head to our hearts. Too often we know about God with our head, but we fail to use that knowledge to really get to know Him with our heart. What God desires is for us to seek after Him with all of our hearts, not just with our minds.

1. What caused Howard Carter to break down and cry when they finally found King Tut's tomb?

    _____

    _____

    _____

2. How might Carter's life been different if he had found the tomb 10 years earlier?

    _____

    _____

    _____

    _____

3. What does it mean to know God with just your head?

    _____

    _____

    _____

    _____

4. What is the difference between knowing God with your head and knowing Him with your heart?

    _____

    _____

    _____

    _____

5. What keeps people from seeking God with their hearts?

    _____

    _____

    _____

    _____

6. In Romans 10:9-10, Paul writes, "If you confess with your mouth, 'Jesus is Lord,' and believe in your heart that God raised him from the dead, you will be saved. For it is with your heart that you believe and are justified, and it is with your mouth that you confess and are saved." How does a person need to know God to have a relationship with Him?

    _____

    _____

    _____

    _____

7. What does God promise to the person who believes with his or her heart that "Jesus is Lord"?

    _____

    _____

    _____

    _____

reflect

1. Think about your current relationship with God. How would you rate it on a scale of 1 to 10?

1	2	3	4	5	6	7	8	9	10

Needs Work   Doing Well

2. What things, if any, keep you from becoming more intimate with God?

   _____

   _____

   _____

   _____

3. Which of the three areas we looked at today—radical brokenness, hunger for God and having a heart for God and
   His work—do you need to work at the most? What will
   you do to better develop your relationship with God in
   those areas?

   _____

   _____

   _____

   _____

4. What are some of the benefits of having a real and intimate
   relationship with God as opposed to having a "religion"?

   _____

   _____

   _____

   _____

5. It's one thing to understand that God calls each of us into
   a more intimate relationship with Himself, but another to
   actually begin to put a plan into effect. In the space below,
   brainstorm several ways in which you can develop your relationship with Christ through: (1) God's Word, (2) prayer,
   (3) worship, and (4) service. An example has been provided
   for each to get you started:

God's word

1. <u>Start having a regular Bible study time</u>
2.
3.
4.

prayer

1. <u>Pray daily</u>
2.
3.
4.

worship

1. <u>Attend worship services regularly at church</u>
2.
3.
4.

service

1. <u>Serve in an area of ministry in your church</u>
2.
3.
4.

Now go back and circle one option in each category. During the next few weeks, make those a regular part of your life.

meditation

Neither death nor life . . . nor anything else in all creation,
will be able to separate us from the love of God.

ROMANS 8:38-39

acts: the life-changing power of God

After [Jesus'] suffering, he showed himself to these men and
gave many convincing proofs that he was alive.

ACTS 1:3

"The proof is in the pudding," the kitchen axiom goes. It all depends on how it tastes when the stove has cooled and the pudding is served. The Acts of the Apostles is the bridge between the good news revealed in the historic human life of Jesus Christ and the Church-guiding and Church-building epistles. The book of Acts is Christianity's "proof in the pudding."

Acts offers the Church four vital aspects of the faith: (1) the proof of the historic launching of the Church, (2) the apologetics of the faith to both Jews and Gentiles, (3) the guidebook by which to live as a follower of Christ, and (4) the triumph of Christianity as a work of God's power more than a manmade religion.

In Acts 4, we read how Peter and John were brought before the religious leaders in Jerusalem for proclaiming their faith in Christ. Peter and John created quite an uproar when they began to testify about the power and presence of the risen Jesus Christ. The high priest and his family inquired as to the source of Peter's and John's power. Peter gave direct attention to Jesus Christ of Nazareth, the Man crucified and now resurrected, as the source of salvation and healing for humanity. After this, "when they [the religious leaders] saw the courage of Peter and John and realized that they were un-schooled, ordinary men, they were astonished and they took note that these men had been with Jesus" (Acts 4:13).

Peter, the same man who we saw in session 1 sink like a rock under the pressure of fear, stood strong as a rock in the face of pending incarceration and death. Why? It wasn't his academic acumen or his extraordinary abilities—it was the life-changing power of God filling Peter. The power of the new Church stemmed from some rather ordinary people who had been with Jesus.

Do you find power in your life these days? Do you see the life-transforming power of Christ adding people to your fellowship and healing the crippled around you? The power of God is fleshed out in the acts of His people who spend time in the presence of Christ before doing His work.

Before you launch into more ministry or the next curriculum of teaching, take a few extra moments to be with Jesus. You will be renewed by His presence and reminded of the life-changing power of the bearer of the Church's name, Jesus Christ.

Be assured, if you walk with Him and look to Him and
expect help from Him, He will never fail you.
GEORGE MUELLER

acts: the life-changing power of God

starter

ORDINARY THINGS: Divide students into at least two groups (6 to 8 in a group). Tell them that they are going on a hunt for some specific things. (You may want to limit where they can look.) The first group to find all the items (or the group who has found the most items when the time expires) is the winner. You may want to provide a simple prize for the winners. Provide each group with a list of items. Here is a sample list of items:

- A picture of your mother
- A picture of your pet
- A bad driver's license picture
- An organized purse

Note: You can download this group study guide in 8½" x 11" format at **www.gospellight.com/uncommon/the_new_testament.zip.**

- A paper clip or safety pin
- Four shoelaces tied end to end (without the shoes)
- Someone who works at a fast-food restaurant
- Someone who has met a celebrity
- Someone who graduated a year early
- Pocket lint
- Hairbrush or comb
- House key
- Electronic gadget (music, phone, game)
- Pair of eyeglasses

After a set amount of time, gather the group back together and briefly share their findings and award prizes if desired. Discuss the following questions:

1. Which items would you classify as ordinary?

2. What makes them ordinary?

3. What would it take to make one of these extraordinary?

message

God is in the business of building the Kingdom and changing lives. He is active in our world today, just as He was in the book of Acts. All we need to do is look around to see His handiwork. We can see it in the mountains, hear it in a baby's cry, and see it in a changed life. And God often uses ordinary people to display His power. In the book of Acts, we see three ways demonstrated in which He was at work: (1) in broken people's lives, (2) in seemingly insurmountable situations, and (3) in hardened hearts. Let's look at each of these in turn.

God's power in broken people's lives

In Acts 3:1-10, we read the story of a man who had been crippled since birth. He lacked the hope of ever being healed, but he was about to come face to face with the power of God:

> *One day Peter and John were going up to the temple at the time of prayer—at three in the afternoon. Now a man crippled from birth was being carried to the temple gate called Beautiful, where he was put every day to beg from those going into the temple courts. When he saw Peter and John about to enter, he asked them for money. Peter looked straight at him, as did John. Then Peter said, "Look at us!" So the man gave them his attention, expecting to get something from them.*
>
> *Then Peter said, "Silver or gold I do not have, but what I have I give you. In the name of Jesus Christ of Nazareth, walk." Taking him by the right hand, he helped him up, and instantly the man's feet and ankles became strong. He jumped to his feet and began to walk. Then he went with them into the temple courts, walking and jumping, and praising God. When all the people saw him walking*

and praising God, they recognized him as the same man who used to sit begging at the temple gate called Beautiful, and they were filled with wonder and amazement at what had happened to him.

1. How did Peter respond to the man's request for money?

    ----

2. How did the crippled man respond to the healing?

    ----

3. By his community's standards, Peter was an ordinary person. But Peter was willing to give what he had to the man in Jesus' name. How do you think the man's life changed because Peter was willing to be used by God?

God's power in changing circumstances

Not only is God in the business of changing lives, but He is also in the business of changing circumstances and freeing people. Often our circumstances present us with difficulties that seem impossible for us to handle, but we need to remember that God has the power to break us out of any situation. We see an example of this in the story of Peter's imprisonment in Acts 12:5-11:

So Peter was kept in prison, but the church was earnestly praying to God for him. The night before Herod was to bring him to trial, Peter was sleeping between two soldiers, bound with two chains, and sentries stood guard at the entrance. Suddenly an angel of the Lord appeared and a light shone in the cell. He struck Peter on the side and woke him up. "Quick, get up!" he said, and the chains fell off Peter's wrists. Then the angel said to him, "Put on your clothes and sandals." And Peter did so. "Wrap your cloak around you and follow me," the angel told him. Peter followed him out of the prison, but he had no idea that what the angel was doing was really happening; he thought he was seeing a vision. They passed the first and second guards and came to the iron gate leading to the city. It opened for them by itself, and they went through it. When they had walked the length of one street, suddenly the angel left him. Then Peter came to himself and said, "Now I know without a doubt that the Lord sent his angel and rescued me from Herod's clutches and from everything the Jewish people were anticipating."

1. How did God respond to the prayers of His people on Peter's behalf?

    _____

    _____

    _____

    _____

2. Why do you think Peter thought he was seeing a vision? When did he realize God had freed him?

    _____

    _____

    _____

    _____

3. What conclusion did Peter come to when he realized he
   was free?

God's power to change hearts

Finally, God also has the power to break into a hard heart to
change it. In Acts 15:25-35, we read of how Paul and Silas sang
hymns of praise to God while in prison. When God then breaks
the two men out of prison, not only does He shake the walls of
the prison but He also shakes the walls of their jailer's heart:

*About midnight Paul and Silas were praying and singing hymns
to God, and the other prisoners were listening to them. Suddenly
there was such a violent earthquake that the foundations of the
prison were shaken. At once all the prison doors flew open, and
everybody's chains came loose. The jailer woke up, and when he
saw the prison doors open, he drew his sword and was about to kill
himself because he thought the prisoners had escaped. But Paul
shouted, "Don't harm yourself! We are all here!"*

*The jailer called for lights, rushed in and fell trembling before
Paul and Silas. He then brought them out and asked, "Sirs, what
must I do to be saved?"*

*They replied, "Believe in the Lord Jesus, and you will be
saved—you and your household." Then they spoke the word of the
Lord to him and to all the others in his house. At that hour of the
night the jailer took them and washed their wounds; then immediately he and all his family were baptized. The jailer brought them
into his house and set a meal before them; he was filled with joy because he had come to believe in God—he and his whole family.*

1. Paul and Silas were stripped, beaten and put into stocks
    before they started singing and praying. What does this
    response say about their hearts for God?

    _____

    _____

    _____

    _____

2. The jailer would have been executed if the prisoners had
    escaped under his watch. How did the jailer first respond
    to what happened in the jail that night?

    _____

    _____

    _____

3. How was the jailer's heart changed when Paul and Silas
    shared Christ with him? Who else was changed?

    _____

    _____

    _____

    _____

dig

People often go through life crippled or chained in body and
spirit. They are desperately begging for direction and healing.
Maybe that's you, or someone you know. Everyone is in need of
the life-changing power of God.

1. How was the power of God displayed in each of the above stories?

2. What are some ways God displays His power today?

3. What attitudes and responses toward God did the people in these stories of Scripture have in common?

4. What does the story of the crippled man tell you about God's ability to use ordinary people?

5. God did not keep Peter, Paul and Silas from ending up in prison or, at times, being physically hurt. How do these stories show us that God's purposes are not necessarily fo-

cused on resolving difficult circumstances? What do you think God's goal is when He changes a circumstance?

6. What was the common ingredient that put the power of God in motion in the story of Peter's imprisonment (Acts 12:5-11) and Paul and Silas's imprisonment (Acts 16:25-34)?

apply

1. God wants to bring life-changing power to our world. He used the obedience of ordinary people like Peter, Paul and Silas, and He does the same today. Yet why is it sometimes difficult to see the power of God working in our lives?

2. When Peter was in prison, the soldiers had him bound in chains. What are some issues or situations that bind teenagers today, making it seem impossible to escape?

3. Why is it tough to look past our circumstances to the power of God?

_____

_____

_____

_____

4. Why does God sometimes choose not to change our circumstances?

_____

_____

_____

_____

5. Prayer can help us see God's power working in our lives. In Philippians 4:6-7, Paul says, "Do not be anxious about anything, but in everything, by prayer and petition, with thanksgiving, present your requests to God. And the peace of God, which transcends all understanding, will guard your hearts and your minds in Christ Jesus." What attitude do we need to have when we pray?

_____

_____

_____

_____

6. What are the characteristics of a changed heart?

_____

_____

_____

_____

7. Why does God sometimes need to break our hearts for change to happen?

_____

_____

_____

_____

reflect

1. The story of Peter, Paul and Silas teaches us that when we place our confidence in God, we will see His power at work in our lives. Circumstances (even painful ones) become opportunities for God to work. How would you answer Jesus if He asked you, "What do you want me to do for you?"

_____

_____

_____

_____

2. Where do you see God working in your life today?

_____

_____

_____

_____

3. How do you measure God's love and interest in your circumstances?

_____

_____

_____

_____

4. What, if anything, keeps you from placing your confidence in God when you have a need?

    _____

    _____

    _____

    _____

    _____

5. To experience change in your life, you need prayer and a plan to pursue. Look at the three areas listed above and spend some time in prayer, asking God to help make a change in your life. Next, take a moment to write out a plan for some things that must happen before that change can occur in your life.

    _____

    _____

    _____

    _____

    _____

    _____

Take a few minutes and ask God to give you the strength to pursue your plan. Ask Him to act powerfully in your life!

meditation

Great is our Lord and mighty in power; his
understanding has no limit.

PSALM 147:5

the letters: the owner's manual

But we have the mind of Christ.

1 CORINTHIANS 2:16

Are you a good instructions-manual type of person? Or do you immediately abandon the instructions to the trash and strike out on your own? Or perhaps you fall somewhere in the middle—you have an undefined but clear statute of limitations that reaches a point of disinterest after a period of time. At some point, you will say to yourself, *Oh, forget it. Following these instructions is just too confusing. I'll just take it and make it work.* Undoubtedly, the typical result is that you end up breaking something and have to spend twice as much time and money for repairs!

So, which of the three roads do you take? Are you . . . (1) An instructions junkie? (2) A glance-and-go-getter? (3) An abandon-and-attack animal?

If you're not sure, take a quick glance at the Blu-Ray player in your home. If the clock is flashing 12:00, you're definitely not a number one. Now play the scene depicting your faith and ministry leadership. Which of the above three levels describes your study of God's Word?

The letters of the apostles serve as the guidebook or instruction manual to a growing faith in Christ. On numerous occasions, Paul speaks of believers as being "in Christ," which is every believer's position before our Holy God. What does it mean to be in Christ? It means to put your life in Jesus and His life in you, taking on not only His presence and His name but also His very mind. Can you think of a more incredible reality than obtaining the mind of Christ?

Read Paul's words to the believers in Corinth in 1 Corinthians 2:16. Then read his words to the Romans in Romans 11:34 and 12:2. Still not convinced you can have the mind of Jesus? Check out Paul's letter to the church at Philippi in Philippians 2:5.

The New Testament letters won't teach you how to change your flashing clock or how to use a spell check program, but they are the owner's manual to your faith. Our purpose is not to become more educated owners but to learn to think, pray, believe, act and live like Christ, the owner of our Christian lives.

So the next time your life hits a flashing point and you feel like you're wasting time, drop the tools and pick up the manual. Read a letter from your Owner to you. You're bound to rebound and find the right way to program this thing called life.

Education is what you get from reading the small print in a contract.
Experience is what you get from not reading it.
ANONYMOUS

the letters: the owner's manual

starter

INVENTORY OF LOVE: One of the primary themes running throughout the letters of the New Testament is the need for us to love God and to love others. On each of the following scales below, circle where you are according to each statement, with 1 meaning that you need some work in this area and 10 meaning that you are doing great.

I regularly tell God how much I love Him.

1	2	3	4	5	6	7	8	9	10
	Needs Work						Doing Great		

Note: You can download this group study guide in 8¹/₂" x 11" format at **www.gospellight.com/uncommon/the_new_testament.zip.**

I spend time with God in His Word on a regular basis.

1	2	3	4	5	6	7	8	9	10

Needs Work   **Doing Great**

I understand what it means to love God.

1	2	3	4	5	6	7	8	9	10

Needs Work   **Doing Great**

My love for God impacts how I treat others.

1	2	3	4	5	6	7	8	9	10

Needs Work   **Doing Great**

I have a hard time loving others.

1	2	3	4	5	6	7	8	9	10

Needs Work   **Doing Great**

I seek to be others-centered.

1	2	3	4	5	6	7	8	9	10

Needs Work   **Doing Great**

I regularly reach out to try to help those in need.

1	2	3	4	5	6	7	8	9	10

Needs Work   **Doing Great**

message

Everyone loves getting mail, whether that is in the form of snail mail, email, a Facebook message or a text message. There's just something about getting a sentiment addressed specifically to you. In the same way, some of the most exciting and memorable parts of the New Testament are the letters. These letters were written by those who knew Jesus and were meant to provide an instruction manual for believers on how to live out their faith and relationship with God on a daily basis.

One of the greatest themes in the letters is loving God and loving others—a theme that launches off Jesus' statement in Matthew 22:37-39: " 'Love the Lord your God with all your heart and with all your soul and with all your mind.' This is the first and greatest commandment. And the second is like it: 'Love your neighbor as yourself.' " Let's explore each of these two commandments in greater detail to determine what it really means to love God and love our neighbors as ourselves.

loving God

The following passages, written in a letter by John, show us what hearts that love God should look like:

> *We know that we have come to know him if we obey his commands. The man who says, "I know him," but does not do what he commands is a liar, and the truth is not in him. But if anyone obeys his word, God's love is truly made complete in him. This is how we know we are in him: Whoever claims to live in him must walk as Jesus did* (1 John 2:3-6).
>
> *This is how we know that we love the children of God: by loving God and carrying out his commands. This is love for God: to obey*

his commands. And his commands are not burdensome, for every-one born of God overcomes the world. This is the victory that has overcome the world, even our faith (1 John 5:2-4).

1. What words do you notice are repeated in these passages?

   _____

   _____

   _____

2. What is "in" the person who knows God?

   _____

   _____

   _____

3. How do these passages describe true love for God?

   _____

   _____

   _____

   _____

4. If we love God, why won't His commandments seem bur-densome to us?

   _____

   _____

   _____

   _____

5. What does it mean to "walk as Jesus did" (1 John 2:6)?

_____

_____

_____

_____

loving others

The response to our love relationship with God is showing His love to others. Paul and John, in their letters to believers, show us what God's love looks like when it is shared with others:

> _Let no debt remain outstanding, except the continuing debt to love one another, for he who loves his fellowman has fulfilled the law. The commandments, "Do not commit adultery," "Do not murder," "Do not steal," "Do not covet," and whatever other commandment there may be, are summed up in this one rule: "Love your neighbor as yourself." Love does no harm to its neighbor. Therefore love is the fulfillment of the law_ (Romans 13:8-10).

> _If you have any encouragement from being united with Christ, if any comfort from his love, if any fellowship with the Spirit, if any tenderness and compassion, then make my joy complete by being like-minded, having the same love, being one in spirit and purpose. Do nothing out of selfish ambition or vain conceit, but in humility consider others better than yourselves. Each of you should look not only to your own interests, but also to the interests of others_ (Philippians 2:1-4).

> _This is how we know what love is: Jesus Christ laid down his life for us. And we ought to lay down our lives for our brothers. If anyone has material possessions and sees his brother in need but has no pity on him, how can the love of God be in him? Dear chil-_

dren, let us not love with words or tongue but with actions and in truth (1 John 3:16-18).

1. In the Romans passage, what debt does Paul describe?

2. What does Paul mean when he says that all of the commandments can be summed up by one simple rule: "Love your neighbor as yourself"?

3. In Philippians 2:4, Paul tells us to look out for the interests of others. What should be our motivation in doing this?

4. What is the difference between loving "with words or tongue" and "with actions and in truth"?

dig

The foundation of the Christian life is about loving God. When we love God, we are changed people. We think, walk and love like God. We have the mind of Christ, and our attitude becomes the same as that of Jesus our Lord (see 1 Corinthians 2:16; Philippians 2:5).

1. How would you describe what it means to love God?

   ....

   ....

   ....

2. First John 2:3-6 says that God's love can live in us and we can live in Him. What is the connection between God's love in us and our ability to live in Him?

   ....

   ....

   ....

3. What are some of the ways that we can walk as Jesus did?

   ....

   ....

   ....

4. How would you describe what it means to love others?

   ....

   ....

   ....

5. How does God help us overcome the world (see 1 John 5:2-4)? What do you think we are overcoming?

_____

_____

_____

_____

6. Which is more difficult: loving God or loving others? Why?

_____

_____

_____

_____

apply

Sometimes, loving others involves a sacrifice on our part. Consider the following story about one such man who was willing to give everything to demonstrate God's love:

In the fourth century, there lived a monk named Telemachus who spent most of his life in a remote community of prayer, raising vegetables for the cloister kitchen. When he was not tending his garden spot, he was fulfilling his vocation of study and prayer.

One day, this monk felt that the Lord wanted him to go to Rome, the capital of the world. Telemachus had no idea why he should go there, and he was terrified at the thought. But as he prayed, God's directive became clear.

Obediently, he left his village in Asia Minor and traveled to Rome. He arrived during the holiday festival, and the city was bustling with excitement over the recent Roman victory over the Goths. In the midst of this jubilant commotion, Telemachus looked for clues as to why God had brought him there, for he had no other guidance, not even a superior in a religious order to contact.

So Telemachus let the crowds guide him, and he was soon led into the Colosseum where the gladiator contests were to be staged. The monk could hear the cries of the animals in their cages beneath the floor of the great arena and the clamor of the contestants preparing to do battle. Then the gladiators marched into the arena, saluted the emperor and shouted, "We who are about to die salute thee!" Telemachus shuddered. He had never heard of the gladiator games before, but he had a premonition of awful violence.

The crowd had come to cheer men who, for no reason other than amusement, would murder each other. Human lives were offered for entertainment. As the monk watched these events unfold, he realized that he could not sit still and watch such savagery. Neither could he leave and forget. He jumped to the top of the perimeter wall and cried, "In the name of Christ, forbear!"

The fighting began, of course. No one paid the slightest heed to him. So Telemachus went down the stone steps and leapt onto the sandy floor of the arena. One gladiator sent him sprawling with a blow from his shield, directing him back to his seat. It was a rough gesture, though almost a kind one. The crowd roared.

But Telemachus refused to stop. He rushed into the way of those trying to fight, shouting again, "In the name of Christ, forbear!" The crowd began to laugh and cheer him on, perhaps thinking him part of the entertainment.

Then his movement blocked the vision of one of the contestants. The gladiator raised his sword and with a flash of steel struck Telemachus, slashing down across his chest and into his stomach. The little monk gasped once more, "In the name of Christ, forbear."

Then a strange thing happened. As the two gladiators and the crowd focused on the fallen body of the monk, the arena grew deathly quiet. In the silence, someone on the top tier got up and walked out. Another followed. All over the arena, spectators began to leave, until the huge stadium was emptied.

There were other forces at work, of course, but that innocent figure lying in a pool of blood crystallized the opposition, and that was the last gladiatorial contest in the Roman Colosseum. Never again did men kill each other for the crowd's entertainment in the Roman arena.[1]

1. How did Telemachus live out his love for God? How did he live out his love for others?

    _____

    _____

    _____

    _____

2. Consider the impact that Telemachus had on the world. If all believers lived out their faith in the same way, what effect could they have on the world?

    _____

    _____

    _____

    _____

3. What would people think of God if all believers lived out their faith this way?

    _____

    _____

    _____

    _____

4. In order to love your neighbor as yourself, what attitude do you need to have toward yourself? How can this affect the way you love your neighbor (see Philippians 2:1-4)?

    _____

    _____

    _____

    _____

5. What types of things keep us from looking out for the interests of others on a regular basis?

    _____

    _____

    _____

    _____

6. How can we love with actions and truth? What are some of the ways that you can meet the needs of others today?

    _____

    _____

    _____

    _____

reflect

Take a moment and draw two pictures. In the first picture, without using any words, draw what it means to love God. In the second picture, also without using any words, draw what it means to love others. After you have drawn your two pictures, consider the following questions:

1. What are some ways we express our love to God as a family?

2. What are some ways we express our love for each other and others outside our family?

3. What are some ways to build a stronger love relationship with God? What might be standing between you and God?

4. What could your life look like if you had the attitude of Christ? What help do you need from God to do this?

_____

_____

_____

_____

5. On the following scale, circle the number where following God's commandments falls for you in your life.

| 1 | 2 | 3 | 4 | 5 | 6 | 7 | 8 | 9 | 10 |

Burdensome   Joyful

Why did you circle the number you did?

_____

_____

_____

_____

What would make obeying God's commandments a joy?

_____

_____

_____

_____

6. What ways has God demonstrated His love for you?

_____

_____

_____

_____

7. What will you do to give yourself more to God? How will
   you seek help to grow in your love for God and others?

   _____
   _____
   _____
   _____
   _____

8. Who is someone right now in your life that needs your
   love? What will you do to show love to that person?

   _____
   _____
   _____
   _____
   _____

meditation

But the fruit of the Spirit is love, joy, peace, patience,
kindness, goodness, faithfulness, gentleness and self-control.
Against such things there is no law.

GALATIANS 5:22-23

Note

1. Adapted from Charles Colson, *Loving God* (Grand Rapids, MI: Zondervan, 1983), pp. 241-243.

revelation: the hope, encouragement and call

"I am the Alpha and the Omega," says the Lord God, "who is, and who was, and who is to come, the Almighty."

REVELATION 1:8

A radio disc jockey was commenting about a movie that was showing in the theaters. He said that he left the movie early so it ended the way he wanted it to end, rather than allowing the end to be selected by the director. "Why would I want to stick around and see the guy die?" he said. What an interesting way to watch a movie!

Of course, for the radio disc jockey's listeners who had yet to see the movie, the plot was now ruined. After all, would you go ahead and watch the movie if you knew the ending? How about watching a football game or reading a novel if you already knew the final outcome? The thrill would be diminished if you knew that your favorite team lost or knew how the main character overcame his or her adversary in the end.

On the other hand, how would your life be different if you knew that your side would win in the end? How would this reality impact your sense of hope? What encouragement would fill your heart if you thought to yourself, *We're going to make it. I don't have to worry about anything.* Would you respond to a call from the coach of a team who was guaranteed to win? If only life could be so predictable.

The book of Revelation is filled with unique images and was written in a distinct literary form. Interpretation varies within different sects of Christianity, but the overall theme of the book is clear: Christ will return, and God's people will enter an eternal life of glory in His presence. God is what He was from the beginning, the "Alpha," or First, and He is what He will be in the end, the "Omega," or Last. And not only is God steadfast in His holiness throughout history, but He is also almighty. He is both perfectly pure and perfectly all-powerful.

Here's the good news for us believers: God wins in the end! Christ returns, and believers are drawn to Him for eternity. We are called to live in Him now with the hopeful encouragement that someday we will spend forever with Him. That makes living each day by faith an inviting prospect.

Yes, God's story ends "and they lived happily ever after."
HENRIETTA MEARS

revelation: the hope, encouragement and call

starter

TIME IS TICKING: Before the meeting begins, make four to five sets of index cards with the following written on the cards:

Card One:	1 hour
Card Two:	1 week
Card Three:	1 month
Card Four:	1 year
Card Five:	10 years

When the session begins, divide the students into groups of four or five and give each group a set of cards. Have the groups distribute a card to each member in the group without anyone revealing his or her card. Now ask the groups the following question: "What would you do if the world were to end in the time indicated on your card?" Allow time for members to share within their groups.

After a few minutes, bring the whole group together and have a few people share their reactions. Use the following questions to guide the discussion:

1. What were your reactions to the time given to you?

2. How would the time frame affect your life?

3. How would a shorter time frame affect your reaction?

4. We don't know when the world is going to end, but God's Word says there will be an end. What effect might knowing this have on your life today?

message

The book of Revelation is a message of hope, encouragement, judgment and a call to all Christians. Within its pages, we see the scenes of the end of the world, the triumph of God over Satan, the final judgment of the world and the incredible description of what the new heaven and the new earth will be like. The book of Revelation is God's call to His believers to stand firm and be prepared for the return of Christ.

Tradition states that the apostle John wrote Revelation during a time of exile on the island of Patmos. At the time, Christians were suffering severe persecution for their faith, and John wanted these believers to know that God was still in control and that He was directing everything that happens in this world. He wanted Christians to persevere in their faith and look toward the ultimate goal: eternal life with their heavenly Father.

John begins his book by listing seven messages given to seven different churches that existed at the time. These messages contain words of warning, correction and instruction from the risen Christ to the believers in these fellowships. Read each of the portions of John's letter to these churches and then briefly answer the questions that follow.

the church in ephesus

I know your deeds, your hard work and your perseverance. I know that you cannot tolerate wicked men. . . . You have persevered and have endured hardships for my name, and have not grown weary. Yet I hold this against you: You have forsaken your first love. Remember the height from which you have fallen! Repent and do the things you did at first. . . . He who has an ear, let him hear what the Spirit says to the churches. To him who over-comes, I will give the right to eat from the tree of life, which is in the paradise of God (Revelation 2:2-5,7).

1. How does Jesus praise this church?

_____

_____

_____

_____

_____

2. What does He warn them about?

_____

_____

_____

_____

the church in smyrna

I know your afflictions and your poverty—yet you are rich! . . . Do not be afraid of what you are about to suffer. I tell you, the devil will put some of you in prison to test you, and you will suffer per-secution for ten days. Be faithful, even to the point of death, and I will give you the crown of life. He who overcomes will not be hurt at all by the second death (Revelation 2:9-11).

1. How does Jesus respond to these believers' suffering?

_____

_____

_____

_____

2. What hope does Jesus give to them?

_____

_____

_____

_____

the church in pergamum

You remain true to my name. You did not renounce your faith in me, even in the days of Antipas, my faithful witness, who was put to death in your city—where Satan lives. Nevertheless, I have a few things against you: You have people there . . . eating food sacrificed to idols and . . . committing sexual immorality. . . . Repent therefore! Otherwise, I will soon come to you and will fight against them with the sword of my mouth. . . . To him who overcomes, I will give some of the hidden manna. I will also give him a white stone with a new name written on it, known only to him who receives it (Revelation 2:13-14,16-17).

1. How does Jesus praise this church?

_____

_____

_____

_____

2. What problem does He tell them they need to address?

_____

_____

_____

_____

the church in thyatira

I know your deeds, your love and faith, your service and persever-
ance, and that you are now doing more than you did at first. Never-
theless, I have this against you: You tolerate that woman Jezebel . . .
she misleads my servants into sexual immorality and the eating of
food sacrificed to idols. . . . Now I say to the rest of you in Thyatira,
to you who do not hold to her teaching and have not learned Sa-
tan's so-called deep secrets . . . hold on to what you have until I
come. To him who overcomes and does my will to the end, I will
give authority over the nations . . . just as I have received authority
from my Father (Revelation 2:19-20,24-27).

1. How does Jesus praise this church?

    ....
    ....
    ....
    ....

2. What warning does He give to them?

    ....
    ....
    ....
    ....

the church in sardis

I know your deeds; you have a reputation of being alive, but you
are dead. Wake up! Strengthen what remains and is about to die,
for I have not found your deeds complete in the sight of my God.
Remember, therefore, what you have received and heard; obey it,

and repent. But if you do not wake up, I will come like a thief, and you will not know at what time I will come to you. Yet you have a few people in Sardis who have not soiled their clothes. They will walk with me, dressed in white, for they are worthy. He who overcomes will, like them, be dressed in white. I will never blot out his name from the book of life, but will acknowledge his name before my Father and his angels (Revelation 3:1-5).

1. What was missing from these believers' faith?

_____

_____

_____

_____

2. What promise does He give those whose faith is genuine?

_____

_____

_____

_____

the church in philadelphia

I know your deeds. . . . I know that you have little strength, yet you have kept my word and have not denied my name. . . . Since you have kept my command to endure patiently, I will also keep you from the hour of trial that is going to come upon the whole world to test those who live on the earth. I am coming soon. Hold on to what you have, so that no one will take your crown. Him who overcomes I will make a pillar in the temple of my God. Never again will he leave it. I will write on him the name of my God and the name of the city of my God, the new Jerusalem, which is coming down out of heaven from my God; and I will also write on him my new name (Revelation 3:8,10-12).

1. How does Jesus encourage the believers in this church?

_____

_____

_____

2. What does He promise them?

_____

_____

_____

_____

the church in laodicea

I know your deeds, that you are neither cold nor hot. I wish you were either one or the other! . . . You say, "I am rich; I have acquired wealth and do not need a thing." But you do not realize that you are wretched, pitiful, poor, blind and naked. Those whom I love I rebuke and discipline. So be earnest, and repent. Here I am! I stand at the door and knock. If anyone hears my voice and opens the door, I will come in and eat with him, and he with me. To him who overcomes, I will give the right to sit with me on my throne, just as I overcame and sat down with my Father on his throne (Revelation 3:15,17-19).

1. What warning does Jesus give this church?

_____

_____

_____

2. What promise does He give to those who repent and turn to Him?

    ---

dig

We should be in awe of God's grace to save each of us from our sin and His power over the evil forces of Satan. We need to be encouraged in the hope of this victory and be ready for it to come!

be encouraged

The seven churches in Revelation faced great challenges: poverty, sin, false teaching, persecution and hypocrisy. Yet Christ offers hope in each situation.

1. Read 1 John 3:2-3. What encouragement does this passage offer for the future and for today?

    ---

2. In Revelation 4:1-8, John describes seeing God on His throne in heaven. What do you think it would be like to see God face to face?

    ---

3. What would you say to Him?

4. The Bible ends with a message of warning and hope for people of every generation. Jesus is victorious, and all evil is vanquished forever:

Then I saw a new heaven and a new earth, for the first heaven and the first earth had passed away, and there was no longer any sea. I saw the Holy City, the new Jerusalem, coming down out of heaven from God, prepared as a bride beautifully dressed for her husband. And I heard a loud voice from the throne saying, "Now the dwelling of God is with men, and he will live with them. They will be his people, and God himself will be with them and be their God. He will wipe every tear from their eyes. There will be no more death or mourning or crying or pain, for the old order of things has passed away." He who was seated on the throne said, "I am making everything new!" Then he said, "Write this down, for these words are trustworthy and true." He said to me: "It is done. I am the Alpha and the Omega, the Beginning and the End. To him who is thirsty I will give to drink without cost from the spring of the water of life. He who overcomes will inherit all this, and I will be his God and he will be my son."

Based on this passage, how would you describe the hope that believers can have for the future?

be ready

We don't know when Jesus will return. It could be today, or it could be years from now. The important point is that we need to be ready at all times for the day of Christ's return.

1. What does Mark 13:35-37 say about how we should live as we wait for Jesus?

    _____

    _____

    _____

    _____

2. What does it mean to "not be caught sleeping"?

    _____

    _____

    _____

    _____

3. What is the reward for those who follow God's Word (see Revelation 22:17)?

    _____

    _____

    _____

    _____

4. What attitude are God's people to have when they look to the future?

    _____

    _____

    _____

    _____

apply

How you look at the future will impact your life for the better today. In addition, the way in which you view the hope of your future can have a positive effect on those who do not yet know Christ.

1. What are some things that distract us from being alert?

2. What can we do to stay awake, keep watch and be alert?

3. What are some things we can do to encourage each other as we see the day approaching?

4. How does Christ's return impact your attitude toward your non-Christian friends and family members?

reflect

What is your immediate reaction when you consider Christ's return? Place a checkmark by the words that describe your feelings.

☐ Thankful	☐ Unworthy
☐ Relieved	☐ Complete
☐ Valuable	☐ Scared
☐ Awe-filled	☐ Unprepared
☐ Renewed	☐ _____
☐ Amazed	☐ _____

1. How will your life be different because of the hope you find in the book of Revelation?

   _____

   _____

   _____

   _____

2. In what areas do you need to be more alert?

   _____

   _____

   _____

   _____

3. What will need to change in your life for you to be ready for His return?

   _____

   _____

   _____

   _____

4. What sense of urgency do you have in sharing Christ with those who don't have a future hope?

_____

_____

_____

_____

5. Take a minute and write a note to God expressing your thanks for the encouragement He gives and to prepare your heart to be ready for His return. Ask for His help in sharing the hope you have with others.

Dear God,

_____

_____

_____

_____

_____

Love always,

_____

meditation

The Spirit and the bride say, "Come!" And let him who hears say, "Come!" Whoever is thirsty, let him come; and whoever wishes, let him take the free gift of the water of life.

REVELATION 22:7

HOME HW WORD

WHERE PARENTS GET REAL ANSWERS

Get Equipped with HomeWord...

LISTEN
HomeWord Radio
programs reach over 800 communities nationwide with *HomeWord with Jim Burns* – a daily ½ hour interview feature, *HomeWord Snapshots* – a daily 1 minute family drama, and *HomeWord this Week* – a ½ hour weekend edition of the daily program, and our one-hour program.

CLICK
HomeWord.com
provides advice and resources to millions of visitors each year. A truly interactive website, HomeWord.com provides access to parent newsletter, Q&As, online broadcasts, tip sheets, our online store and more.

READ
HomeWord Resources
parent newsletters, equip families and Churches worldwide with practical Q&As, online broadcasts, tip sheets, our online store and more. Many of these resources are also packaged digitally to meet the needs of today's busy parents.

ATTEND
HomeWord Events
Understanding Your Teenager, Building Healthy Morals & Values, Generation 2 Generation and Refreshing Your Marriage are held in over 100 communities nationwide each year. HomeWord events educate and encourage parents while providing answers to life's most pressing parenting and family questions.

A Ministry with *Jim Burns*

In response to the overwhelming needs of parents and families, Jim Burns founded HomeWord in 1985. HomeWord, a Christian organization, equips and encourages parents, families, and churches worldwide.

Find Out More
Sign up for our FREE daily
e-devotional and parent e-newsletter
at HomeWord.com, or call 800.397.9725.

HomeWord.com

Small Group Curriculum Kits

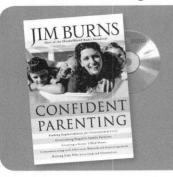

Confident Parenting Kit

This is a must-have resource for today's family! Let Jim Burns help you to tackle overcrowded lives, negative family patterns, while creating a grace-filled home and raising kids who love God and themselves.

Kit contains:
- 6 sessions on DVD featuring Dr. Jim Burns
- CD with reproducible small group leader's guide and participant guides
- poster, bulletin insert, and more

Creating an Intimate Marriage Kit

Dr. Jim Burns wants every couple to experience a marriage filled with A.W.E.: affection, warmth, and encouragement. He shows husbands and wives how to make their marriage a priority as they discover ways to repair the past, communicate and resolve conflict, refresh their marriage spiritually, and more!

Kit contains:
- 6 sessions on DVD featuring Dr. Jim Burns
- CD with reproducible small group leader's guide and participant guides
- poster, bulletin insert, and more

Parenting Teenagers for Positive Results

This popular resource is designed for small groups and Sunday schools. The DVD features real family situations played out in humorous family vignettes followed by words of wisdom by youth and family expert, Jim Burns, Ph.D.

Kit contains:
- 6 sessions on DVD featuring Dr. Jim Burns
- CD with reproducible small group leader's guide and participant guides
- poster, bulletin insert, and more

Teaching Your Children Healthy Sexuality Kit

Trusted family authority Dr. Jim Burns outlines a simple and practical guide for parents on how to develop in their children a healthy perspective regarding their bodies and sexuality. Promotes godly values about sex and relationships.

Kit contains:
- 6 sessions on DVD featuring Dr. Jim Burns
- CD with reproducible small group leader's guide and participant guides
- poster, bulletin insert, and more

Parent and Family Resources from HomeWord for you and your kids...

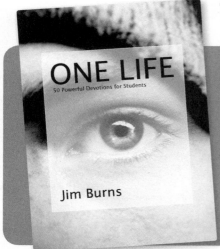

One Life Kit

Your kids only have one life – help them discover the greatest adventure life has to offer! 50 fresh devotional readings that cover many of the major issues of life and faith your kids are wrestling with such as sex, family relationships, trusting God, worry, fatigue and daily surrender. And it's perfect for you and your kids to do together!

Addicted to God Kit

Is your kids' time absorbed by MySpace, text messaging and hanging out at the mall? This devotional will challenge them to adopt thankfulness, make the most of their days and never settle for mediocrity! Fifty days in the Scripture is bound to change your kids' lives forever.

Devotions on the Run Kit

These devotionals are short, simple, and spiritual. They will encourage you to take action in your walk with God. Each study stays in your heart throughout the day, providing direction and clarity when it is most needed.

90 Days Through the New Testament Kit

Downloadable devotional. Author Jim Burns put together a Bible study devotional program for himself to follow, one that would take him through the New Testament in three months. His simple plan was so powerful that he was called to share it with others. A top seller!

Small Group Curriculum Kits

Confirming Your Faith Kit

Rite-of-Passage curriculum empowers youth to make wise decisions...to choose Christ. Help them take ownership of their faith! Lead them to do this by experiencing a vital Christian lifestyle.

Kit contains:
- 13 engaging lessons
- Ideas for retreats and special Celebration
- Solid foundational Bible concepts
- 1 leaders guide and 6 student journals (booklets)

10 Building Blocks Kit

Learn to live, laugh, love, and play together as a family. When you learn the 10 essential principles for creating a happy, close-knit household, you'll discover a family that shines with love for God and one another! Use this curriculum to help equip families in your church.

Kit contains:
- 10 sessions on DVD featuring Dr. Jim Burns
- CD with reproducible small group leader's guide and participant guides
- poster and bulletin insert
- 10 Building Blocks book

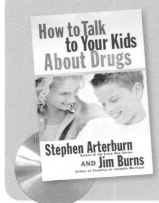

How to Talk to Your Kids About Drugs Kit

Dr. Jim Burns speaks to parents about the important topic of talking to their kids about drugs. You'll find everything you need to help parents learn and implement a plan for drug-proofing their kids.

Kit contains:
- 2 session DVD featuring family expert Dr. Jim Burns
- CD with reproducible small group leader's guide and participant guides
- poster, bulletin insert, and more
- How to Talk to Your Kids About Drugs book

Tons of helpful resources for youth workers, parents and youth. Visit our online store at www.HomeWord.com or call us at 800-397-9725

WHERE PARENTS GET REAL ANSWERS